INTRODUCTION

Having a theme to a party greatly adds to the fun and excitement, and encourages children to join in and use their imaginations.

This section is full of ideas and useful tips, including suggestions for sending invitations, decoration, dressing up, food, games and what to give as going home presents.

Remember to tailor the party to the children attending. Very young children do not enjoy games with complicated rules. In general, keep games simple and vary the pace with quiet games alternating with more boisterous activity. Parties involving different age groups and mixes of boys and girls need careful planning. However much you may wish otherwise, boys and girls may have different ideas about what they want to wear, eat and play.

However, a theme party needn't require extra work on your part, just some forward planning. For example, much of the food can be made in advance and then kept in the freezer or in airtight containers. Children love music, so choose some records or tapes for them to sing and dance to. Try and enlist some extra adult help on the day of the party to ensure everything goes smoothly.

PREPARATION 1

Invitations

This book gives you ideas to help you make party invitations. Why not get the birthday child to help you. This will give you both a fun activity to share.

If you are going to use envelopes, remember to measure them first, so you can make the invitations to fit.

Give invitations out about two weeks before the day - early enough to avoid disappointment on refusal, but not so early that the date gets forgotten!

Make your invitations from brightly coloured paper or card. Keep illustrations simple and uncluttered. If you have access to a photocopying machine you can simply make copies of a drawing, stick them on to coloured paper and colour them in.

Collage is also fun, easy to do and very effective. Cut or tear up old magazines or comics and stick the pictures on to card. Differently sized lettering from old newspapers looks good rearranged to spell out the word 'party'.

On the inside or back of the invitation write the date, place, and starting and finishing times of the party. For small children's parties, an hour and a half is probably long enough. Three hours is a sensible limit for older children.

Please come to JACK'S PARTY on Tuesday 1st March at 26 Valley Road from 3.00pm - 4:00

THE COMPLETE BOOK OF
Children's
PARTIES

C L A R E   B E A T O N

CONTENTS

Kingfisher Books

1 · THEMES

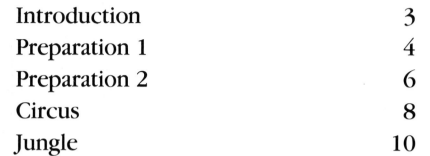

Dressing up

Keep dressing-up clothes simple and comfortable to wear. Improvise with what old clothes you may already have. Alternatively, jumble sales and charity shops are good places to find garments, for example old curtains for cloaks and wings. Make sure they are clean!

You could start a theme party by getting the children to make something to go with their outfits, or a prop for a game. This activity can help guests get over any initial shyness and provide something for them to do while waiting for everyone to arrive.

Have everything laid out on a table ready for the children. Have all masks, badges and hats cut out and ready to be decorated, to avoid children using scissors. Have a good selection of sticky shapes, sequins, feathers, glitter, glue and felt-tip pens set out. Badges are simple to make from circles of card with a safety pin taped to the back.

Decorations

Balloons and streamers always look great at any party. Put a couple of balloons on the front door to emphasize where the party is being held. If you're holding your party outdoors, hang a bunch of balloons from a tree or bench.

For a particularly decorative look, attach a thread or string to the ceiling or walls so that it hangs above the party tea table, then drape streamers over it. You can adapt this idea with your theme in mind, for example thin black plastic streamers and cut-out spiders look great at a monster party.

If you buy balloons, hang them in big bunches for maximum effect. You could then give one to each guest as they leave.

If you want to be more ambitious and reinforce your theme, you can stick cut-out paper shapes to the windows and doors. You could hang ragged black plastic bin liners from doorways at a monster party, tinsel for a fairy party, and green crêpe paper for a jungle party.

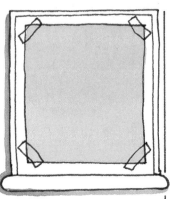

Coloured crêpe or tissue paper taped on to windows will give an unusual light and add to the atmosphere.

You might even get your guests to help with the decorating by colouring in a simple mural with felt-tip pens, outlined on lining paper (or the back of old wallpaper) pinned to a wall. You could start the party this way. It doesn't have to be finished - your own children will enjoy carrying on if you leave it up for a few days.

Continue the theme when decorating the table. For a jungle party you can cover plates or trays with green paper leaves, or use aluminium foil for a space party. Limiting the scheme to just one or two colours is most effective.

Games

Have a list of games and a box of props and small prizes (if you want to give any) all ready before the party. Be prepared for more games than you think you will need. Try not to have gaps between the games as the children will get restless. If the weather permits, hold the party outdoors where there is plenty of space. You could perhaps then have a barbecue party. However, it's always a good idea to have alternative indoor games planned, in case it rains or turns cold.

Adapt the games to fit your theme. For example, rather than have *Pin the tail on the donkey*, you could have *Pin the helmet on the spaceman* at a space party, or *Pin the star on the fairy's wand* at a fairy party.

Treasure hunts are always fun and can be written to a theme with an appropriate prize. Children enjoy hunting for small hidden objects so these could also be chosen with the theme in mind. Hide chocolate coins at a pirate's party and small plastic animals at a jungle party.

Food

Most party food will be the same whatever party you have. But try to include a few things that are in keeping with your theme. Whatever you do, keep it simple, easy to eat, but fun and attractive.

Biscuits and fairy cakes are easy to make using cutters and cake tins. You can make them well in advance to keep in the freezer.

Encourage your child to help you make the food, but discourage the use of too much dark or lurid food colouring as this will look, and be, less appetising.

If you're having a picnic, you can pack up individual boxes (taking extra supplies to top up). Buy the boxes from bakers or use old ice cream tubs.

Cake

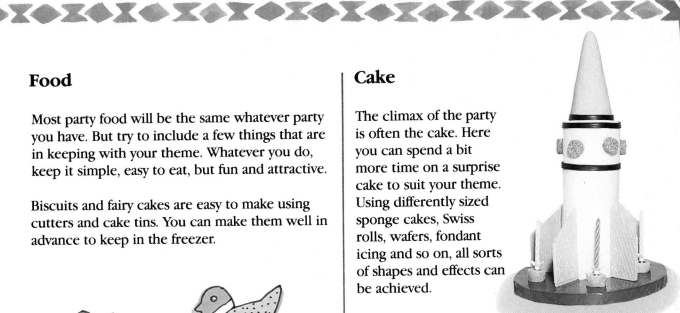

The climax of the party is often the cake. Here you can spend a bit more time on a surprise cake to suit your theme. Using differently sized sponge cakes, Swiss rolls, wafers, fondant icing and so on, all sorts of shapes and effects can be achieved.

If everyone is too full to eat a piece of cake, give out slices, wrapped in paper napkins or tin foil, to take home.

Going Home

Even going home presents can be chosen with the theme in mind. There are endless cheap, small presents and sweets to choose from. If you like you can replace the usual plastic party bags with paper cones, small boxes and so on.

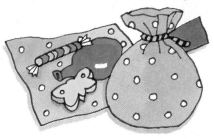

Assemble all the gifts well in advance and keep them together in a box or basket. For a personal touch you could stick on individual name labels.

CIRCUS

INVITATION

Make a Big Top card with opening doors, as shown.

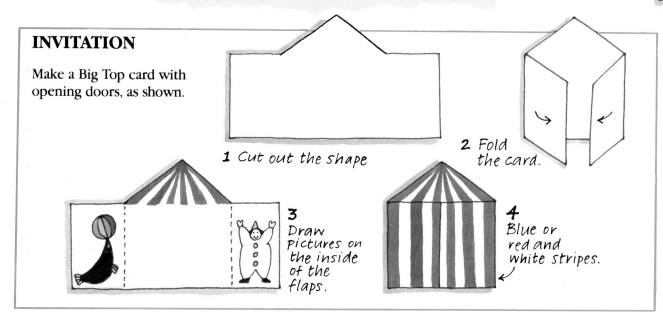

1 Cut out the shape

2 Fold the card.

3 Draw pictures on the inside of the flaps.

4 Blue or red and white stripes.

DRESSING UP

Dress up as a clown, strong man, tightrope walker, acrobat, or ringmaster.

Clown
Mix small and large clothes

Stick on or sew bright patches

Acrobat
Leotard and tights with net frill.

Use face paints for greater effect

Decorated yoghurt pot for hat.

Strongman
Fur fabric suit and card weights

GAMES

- Make your own *Pin the nose on the clown's face.*
- See who can balance an object on their nose for the longest time. You could use a ball or a matchbox.
- Play *Ringmaster says* as a version of 'Simon says'. The ringmaster could wear a top hat.
- *Hoopla:* cut hoops out of cardboard and throw them over mini bags of sweets laid out on the floor.

FOOD

Cut top hat place mats out of paper.

Serve:
- Popcorn.
- Toffee apples.
- Biscuits iced with clown faces, or in the shape of bow ties, 'spotted' with sweets.
  - 'Red noses' made from cherry tomatoes or glacé cherries stuck on biscuits with cheese or icing.

Ball of red fondant icing for nose →

CAKE

Using a round sponge cake, decorate with a clown's face on top of fondant icing.

DECORATIONS

Hang up lots of brightly coloured balloons and streamers.

↗ Cut star shapes out of fondant icing

GOING HOME

At the end of a circus party you could give out giant balloons, party blowers, dolly mixtures, red noses and bubble mixture. Buy or make simple party hats (from large yogurt pots) to put the presents in.

9

JUNGLE

INVITATION

Make an animal-outline stencil.
Cut out the shape or
colour it in.

Snake card

Elephant card

1 Draw the
outline on
card.

2 Cut round
the outline with a craft knife.

3 Tape the stencil over
coloured card. Paint
through the stencil.

DRESSING UP

Choose your animal. Here are some examples:

Parrot - make a bird's head hat with beak, as shown. Add paper wings and a tail. Flippers could be used to look like birds' feet.

Elephant - make large paper ears and a 'tube' trunk and wear a grey tracksuit.

Lion, leopard or tiger - stick spots or stripes on to a leotard. Make ears and a tail. Use face paints to make animal faces.

Crêpe paper frill for mane, attached to ribbon. →

Mane

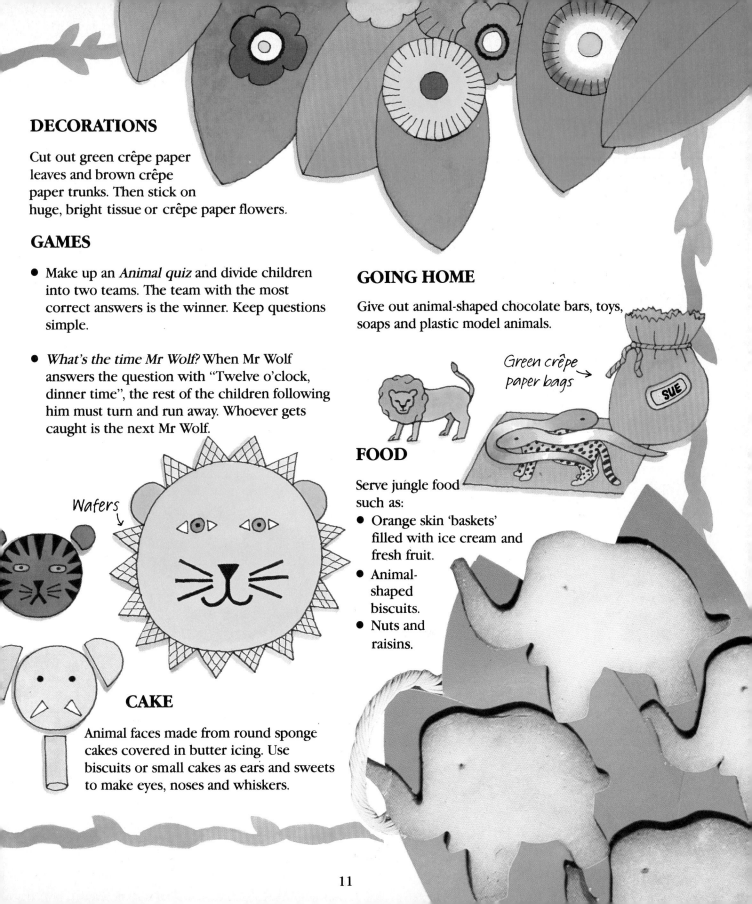

DECORATIONS

Cut out green crêpe paper leaves and brown crêpe paper trunks. Then stick on huge, bright tissue or crêpe paper flowers.

GAMES

- Make up an *Animal quiz* and divide children into two teams. The team with the most correct answers is the winner. Keep questions simple.

- *What's the time Mr Wolf?* When Mr Wolf answers the question with "Twelve o'clock, dinner time", the rest of the children following him must turn and run away. Whoever gets caught is the next Mr Wolf.

Wafers

CAKE

Animal faces made from round sponge cakes covered in butter icing. Use biscuits or small cakes as ears and sweets to make eyes, noses and whiskers.

GOING HOME

Give out animal-shaped chocolate bars, toys, soaps and plastic model animals.

Green crêpe paper bags

SUE

FOOD

Serve jungle food such as:
- Orange skin 'baskets' filled with ice cream and fresh fruit.
- Animal-shaped biscuits.
- Nuts and raisins.

TEDDY'S PICNIC

INVITATION

Make a 'teddy' mask and use it as an invitation.

Trace this shape on to thin card and cut it out.

Write the party details on the back. Add a note asking guests to bring the mask, but have a few extra ready for those who forget.

Thread thin elastic through holes and knot.

DRESSING UP

Ask guests to wear their mask and bring their own teddy with them.

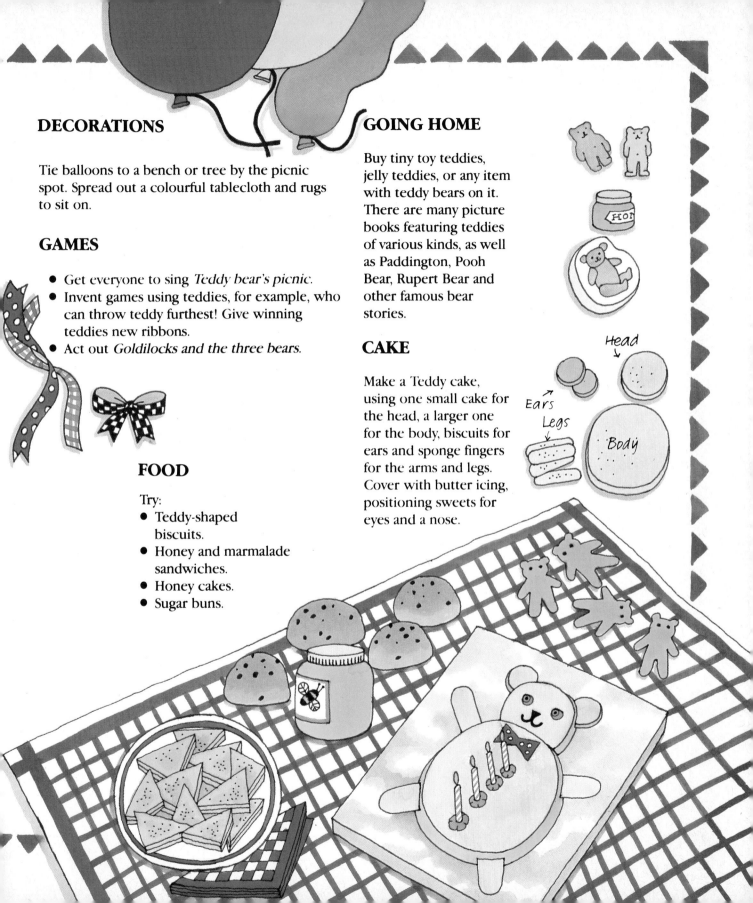

DECORATIONS

Tie balloons to a bench or tree by the picnic spot. Spread out a colourful tablecloth and rugs to sit on.

GAMES

- Get everyone to sing *Teddy bear's picnic.*
- Invent games using teddies, for example, who can throw teddy furthest! Give winning teddies new ribbons.
- Act out *Goldilocks and the three bears.*

FOOD

Try:
- Teddy-shaped biscuits.
- Honey and marmalade sandwiches.
- Honey cakes.
- Sugar buns.

GOING HOME

Buy tiny toy teddies, jelly teddies, or any item with teddy bears on it. There are many picture books featuring teddies of various kinds, as well as Paddington, Pooh Bear, Rupert Bear and other famous bear stories.

CAKE

Make a Teddy cake, using one small cake for the head, a larger one for the body, biscuits for ears and sponge fingers for the arms and legs. Cover with butter icing, positioning sweets for eyes and a nose.

Head

Ears

Legs

Body

MONSTER

Fold in four ↓

Cut

Paint or draw a monster.

INVITATION

A simple monster pop-up card coloured in lurid colours such as black, purple, lime green and orange looks very effective.

'Creepy crawlies' on pipe cleaners fixed to head bands. →

DRESSING UP

Wear black or purple and add any combination of tails, masks, antennae, horns, cloaks, false nails and teeth. Good materials to use include shiny plastic, net and fur. Making up faces with face paints can add the finishing touch.

Flippers ↓

Paper Devil's tail ↓

↙ Black bin liner cloak

Make card mask and add wool hair. ↙

Cardboard mask with elastic ↘

Black stocking mask with paper decorations. →

CAKE

To make a monster cake, place a small pudding basin sponge cake on top of a round sponge cake, and then cover the shape with green runny glacé icing. Use liquorice for hands and mouth, and large sweets for eyes.

FOOD

Serve:
- Sugar 'rats'. ● Purple jelly. ● Small 'spider' sponge cakes or doughnuts with liquorice 'legs'.
- Black and green grapes.

Mashed up black jelly

GAMES

- Blindfold children so that they have to guess by smell and feel what certain unusually textured objects are, for example, cooked spaghetti.

- Let them search with their hands for small objects hidden in mashed up jelly. These games could be messy, so provide aprons and waterproof table covers.

DECORATIONS

Cut black bin liners and crêpe paper into tatters to hang around the room. Cover the windows in tissue paper with shapes cut out. You could make spiders' webs out of black wool. Hang cut-out or plastic spiders from thread strung above the table.

GOING HOME

Give out monster sweets and black balloons. Joke blood is always popular, as are plastic flies and spiders. You could also make simple 'finger' monster puppets.

Tied up black plastic or paper

FAIRY

INVITATION

Cut stars out of silver and gold paper. Then stick glitter on one side and write the party details on the other.

Tape stick to back of star.

Cut a card template to draw round.

Paper star on elastic

Use face paints to decorate your face.

DRESSING UP

Dress in a leotard or pretty vest with a net skirt and white tights.

Length from wrist to wrist with arms held out.

Wings made from net curtain

Elastic loops for wrists

Gather up and tack in position on vest or leotard.

Ballet shoes

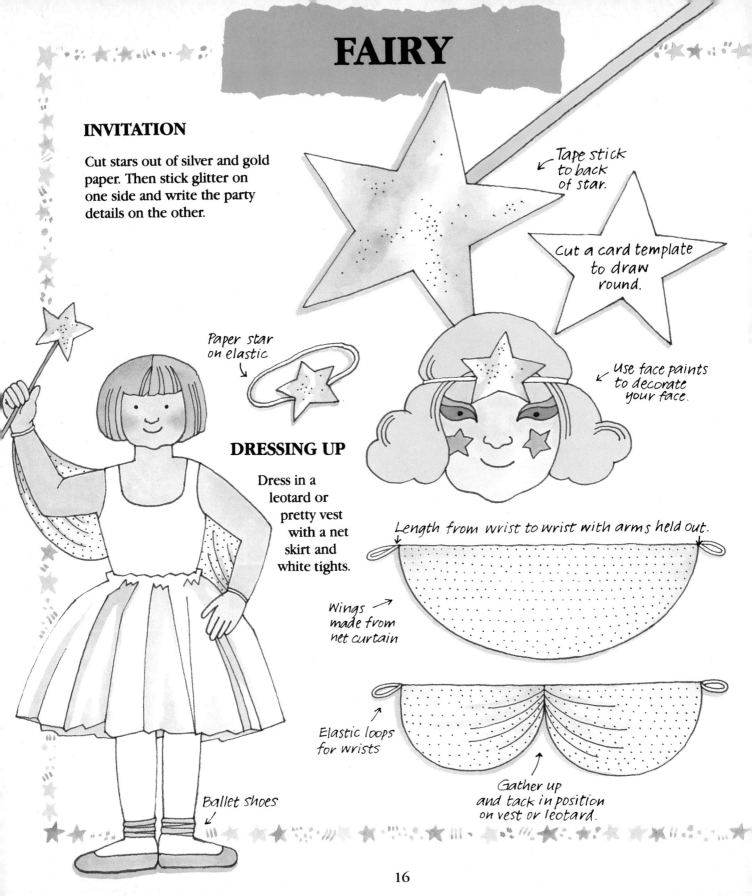

DECORATIONS

Hang tinsel above the table over a string.

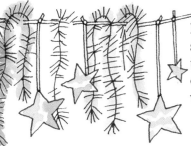

Hang silver and gold stars and moons from the ceiling on threads, or stick them to windows and doors.

CAKE

GAMES

- Dancing to music.

- *Pin the star on the fairy's wand.*

- You could hire a magician to do a magic show.

To make a fairy cake, use a pudding basin sponge cake as a skirt. Model the fairy's body from fondant icing or use a small plastic doll. Cut out paper wings and make a wand from a cocktail stick and two stars stuck together.

GOING HOME

You could make pretty cones out of paper doilies and fill them with sweets wrapped in shiny metallic paper, tiny biscuits and tubes of glitter.

FOOD

Make or buy:
- Tiny iced biscuits.
- Star-shaped decorated biscuits.
- Fairy cakes
- Pastel-coloured meringues stuck together with cream.

SPACE

INVITATION

Cut out rocket or planet shapes from card.

Come to
JOE'S
Party

Emma's Space Party
at
15 The Glade

20th March
from 2:00 pm - 3:00 pm

Colour the shapes in and write the party details on with a silver pen. Then stick on silver and gold stars.

DRESSING UP

Dress in all-in-ones, boiler suits or track suits, adding belts. Stick on badges and wear a helmet which you could make using a hat or crash helmet decorated with stars and symbols.

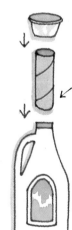

Laser gun made from a plastic bottle, cardboard tube and plastic tub.

Wellington boots

GAMES

- Play *Pass the space parcel*, wrapping the prize in layers of silver paper.

- Hold a competition to see who can draw the best Alien.

CAKE

Paper flag on cocktail stick.

Lego models

Make a 'moon cake' using a pudding basin sponge cake covered with fondant icing. Make jagged holes in the icing for craters. For the finishing touch, stick on toy space men and space buggies.

GOING HOME

There are lots of space theme sweets you could give out, including Mars bars, Milky Ways, Space Dust and Flying Saucers. Or you could give toy rockets, sticky stars, or books about space.

DECORATIONS

Hang up silver foil moons and stars. Buy silver balloons or you could spray ordinary ones with silver spray paint.

FOOD

- Serve individual 'space meals', packed picnic style in named boxes. Include items such as moon rock cakes, and sandwiches wrapped in foil.

☆Joe☆

Cake box or ice cream tub →

Plastic containers of drink →

19

PIRATE

INVITATION

X marks the spot for this party. Cut out an island shape from thick paper and colour one side. Then write the party details on the back. Alternatively, glue or draw a white skull and crossbones on black card.

DRESSING UP

Make pirate pants from old trousers with jagged cut-off legs and patches sewn on. Add stripey T-shirts and spotty handkerchiefs. Or you could make a paper pirate's hat with skull and crossbones.

For the character Long John Silver, hop on one leg and use a wooden stick as a crutch. You could even put a toy parrot on your shoulder.

Hoop earrings sewn to scarf.

Black card eye patch on elastic

Wellington boots or bare feet depending on weather

DECORATIONS

Cut out paper palm trees and add green paper leaves and cut-out or use toy parrots.

GAMES

- Make up a *Treasure hunt* around the house or garden to find hidden chocolate coins.
- Invent a simple secret code, using it to write clues to the whereabouts of 'buried' treasure.

GOING HOME

Chocolate money, small plastic ships, eye patches, sweet necklaces, bracelets and plastic jewellery could make up pirate's treasure. As a novelty, cut up spotty cotton material into squares and tie on to a stick for them to carry it home in.

FOOD

You could serve:
- Boats made from halved bread rolls covered with cream cheese, or peanut butter, with paper sails on cocktail sticks.
- Biscuits iced with skull and crossbones, or wrapped in coloured foil paper to look like jewels.

CAKE

Cut a loaf-shaped sponge cake into a prow at one end. Use brown fondant icing to cover the sides and top. Add sails and flags, using sweets for portholes.

Make sails and flags out of thick paper.

Knitting needles or wooden skewers for masts.

SPOTTY

INVITATION

Decorate a thick paper or card circle with coloured spots. You could write the party details round in a circle, too.

Lightly draw ↗ *guidelines with a pair of compasses to help write your message in a circle.*

Please come to my spotty par on Tuesday 3rd Ma at 96 Th

in the Park at 4:00pm

S P A R

DRESSING UP

Wear spotty clothes, or paint lots of spots on old plain clothes with fabric pens.

Stick adhesive paper circles on to fabric

Alternatives

Or you could have a stripey party or a party with one particular colour, and dress in appropriate clothes.

DECORATIONS

Stick or draw spots on to the tablecloth, walls, paper cups etc. . Thread large paper circles on to ribbons and hang them up as decorations. Or have one colour for everything if you are having a one-colour party.

GOING HOME

Anything circular or spotted would be suitable, for example Smarties, marbles, dice-shaped erasers and sheets of sticky paper spots.

GAMES

- Hold tiddlywink races, making a circular board with a centre target marked on it. The first child to flick a tiddlywink on to the target is the winner.
- Move tiddlywinks from one bowl to another by sucking them up with a straw. The child who moves the most in a given time is the winner.
- Organize a Smarties hunt.

Plastic counters

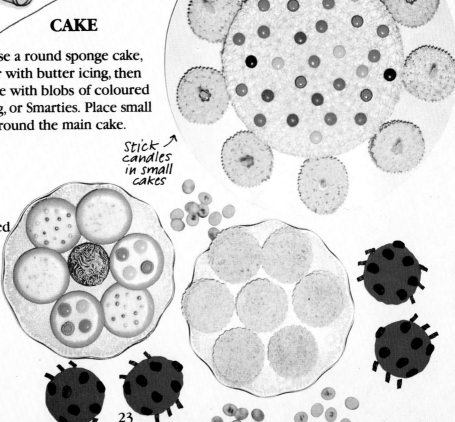

CAKE

Use a round sponge cake, cover with butter icing, then decorate with blobs of coloured glacé icing, or Smarties. Place small fairy cakes around the main cake.

Stick candles in small cakes

FOOD

Serve:
- Round biscuits decorated with round sweets.

- Sandwiches cut into circles with biscuit cutters.

MORE IDEAS

Christmas Party

Cut out Christmas tree-shaped invitations from green paper and stick on coloured spots for baubles and glitter.

- Decorate the party room with balloons, baubles, tinsel, holly and laurel leaves. Edge the food table with tinsel.
- Dress up as Father Christmas, a Christmas fairy, or as a Christmas tree dressed in green with tinsel and baubles attached. Or go as a present dressed in red with ribbons.
- Traditional food and Christmas cake. Or a Christmas log from a Swiss roll covered in chocolate icing and dusted with icing sugar 'snow'.
- For going home presents, give out paper or material stockings filled with nuts and Christmas sweets and a little wrapped present.

Swimming Party

Depending on the guests' ages, a paddling pool may be sufficient. Or go to the local swimming pool. Strictly supervise the children at all times.

- Make invitations in the shape of a swimming pool, or a fish, asking guests to come in beach wear with their swimming gear.
- Play water polo with a ball, and races if you are using a swimming pool; who can throw the rubber ring the furthest, in the water or in the garden; bobbing for apples in a bowl of water.
- Picnic outside on beach towels. Make fish-shaped biscuits and serve ice cream. A loaf tin cake decorated as a swimming pool or cut into a fish shape with wafer fins.

Firework Party

- Cut out firework-shaped invitations.
- Set up a barbecue so that you can eat outdoors.
- Serve baked potatoes, sausages, and hamburgers, toffee apples and popcorn.
- Help children to toast marshmallows and chestnuts on long forks or skewers.
- Have plenty of helpers to organize and supervise the firework display.
- Give each child a sparkler so they can draw patterns or write their name in the air.
- The cake could be made in the shape of a rocket by standing Swiss rolls on end and covering them in icing. Use wafers for wings and an ice cream cone for the nose.

It's a Knockout

Divide guests into two differently coloured teams, or 'spotty' and 'stripey' teams.

- Colour invitations to match - state which team the children are a member of so they come appropriately dressed.
- Hold three-legged races, wheelbarrow races, welly throwing and relay obstacle races.
- Give teams prizes. Have lots of games so each team wins some.
- Serve picnic tea with differently coloured cakes for each team.
- Give out appropriately coloured 'sporty' going home presents.

Party FOOD

2 · FOOD

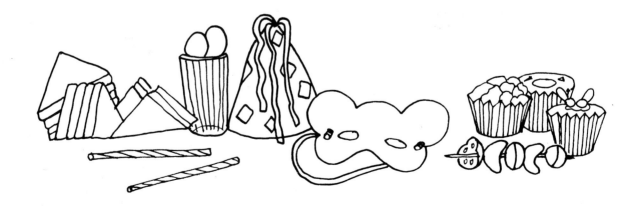

INTRODUCTION

The best party food is fun and easy to eat. Keep ideas simple and colourful. If you are having a party with a theme, you could make some of the food to match.

Sandwiches, biscuits, jelly and ice cream are always popular at any party tea. With the main components of a party tea in mind, this section has been divided into separate topics to give you lots of novel but simple ideas to choose from.

Much of the food can be cooked or prepared in advance, and kept in the freezer or airtight containers. Cakes and biscuits can be iced and decorated the morning before the party.

Many children get too excited at parties to eat large amounts, so don't overdo the quantities. Bite-size 'nibbles' usually go down well with children as they can try a bit of everything.

It's a good idea to have a variety of savoury and sweet things on the table to cater for different tastes. Food cut or arranged in novel shapes will appeal most to children.

It's also a good idea to set individual places at the tea table for each guest. Provide plenty of colourful napkins, as most of the party food will be eaten with their fingers.

Colour is perhaps the most important thing to consider when preparing a party tea. Bright colours always look good, but avoid using too many lurid or dark colours as these will look less appetising.

Natural food colourings are available such as beetroot red, annatto, anthracene, riboflavin and cochineal. When shopping, check ingredients carefully to avoid too many E numbers in the form of artificial colours, preservatives and sweeteners.

Other ingredients to avoid include whole nuts and anything that could get stuck in children's throats. Also beware of serving strong tasting or spicy food to children. It's safer to make simple dishes, then concentrate on decorating and presenting them attractively.

TABLE DECOR

The food table is usually the central attraction of the party, so decorate it with special care. If you are having a party with a theme, it adds to the fun to try and match the table decor and some of the food to it. For example, at a space party you could cover the table and plates with silver foil and dangle cardboard planets and moons from a string strung above the table. However you decide to decorate your table, make sure it is well covered with spillproof material, and always provide plenty of paper napkins.

Place mats

Novelty-shaped individual place mats can be cut out of cardboard or thick paper. Simply use a stencil or tracing, or draw round an appropriate object. Make large circles for a spotty party, or top hats for a circus party and get the children to colour and decorate their own when they arrive.

Place names

To avoid any arguments over where everyone is to sit, it is a good idea to put each guest's name already at a place setting. The birthday child may enjoy writing these on folded pieces of card and perhaps drawing the person's face too. Again, if you are having a theme, you could cut the cards into appropriate shapes.

Plates and cups

You can buy many different kinds of patterned plastic and paper party cups and plates. However, you may prefer to decorate some yourself, with stickers or sticky stars and spots. Do not use spray paints or pens to colour anything that will come in contact with food, as they may be toxic.

Hats and masks

You could make or buy a party hat or mask for each child and have them ready to wear beside their place at the table. These could match your theme if you're having one. Children also love having party blowers and streamers to play with at the table.

Finishing touches

Put bendy straws and paper umbrellas in drinks for a fun touch. Place bite-size pieces of food on cocktail sticks and stick into half grapefruits or oranges for a 'hedgehog' effect. When you are ready for the cake, dim the lights and make a grand entrance with candles alight.

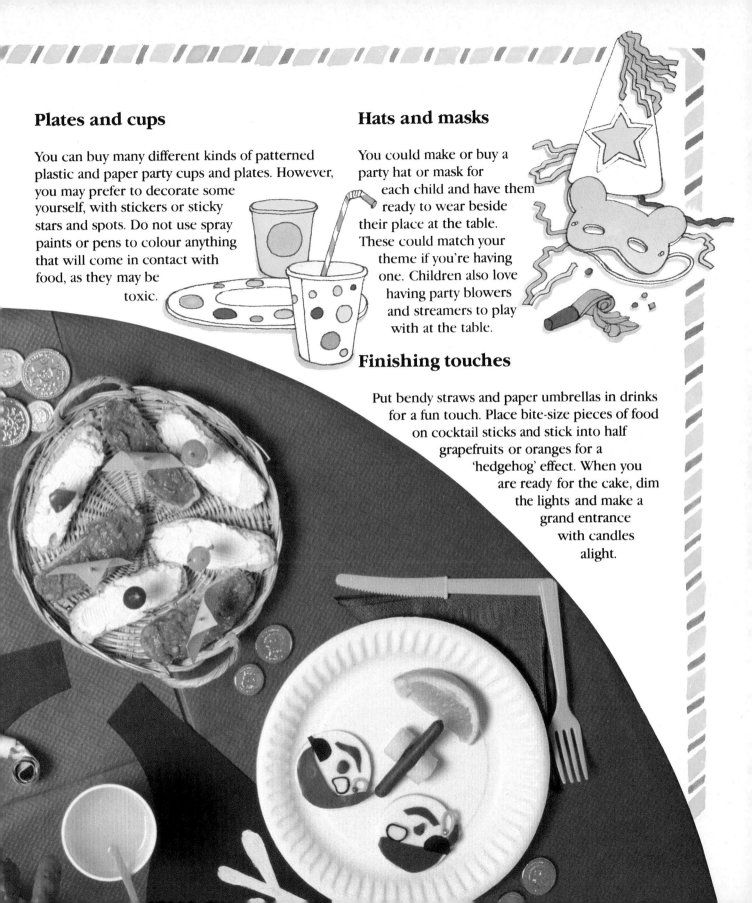

SANDWICHES

Children find sandwiches made from thinly sliced bread easier to eat. Make a variety of different fillings, clearly marked.

Make the sandwiches on the day of the party, keeping them well covered so they don't dry out. Garnish them at the last minute with mustard and cress or twists of cucumber.

There are plenty of novel ways you can serve sandwiches to make them more appealing. Try cutting them into different shapes using biscuit cutters.

SANDWICH WHEELS

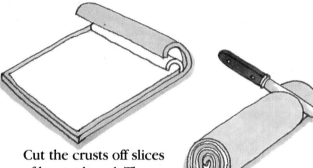

Cut the crusts off slices of brown bread. Then, with a rolling pin, roll the slices out lightly and spread thickly with cream cheese. Place a stick of celery across one end of each slice and roll up tightly. Wrap the rolls in foil until just before eating. Then cut them into 10mm (½ in) slices to serve.

CHESSBOARD

Arrange small squares of brown and white sandwiches like a chessboard.

CROISSANTS

Croissants can be stuffed with sweet or savoury fillings. You could also use bagels and differently flavoured breads. Look out for bakeries or delicatessens selling animal-shaped rolls and loaves.

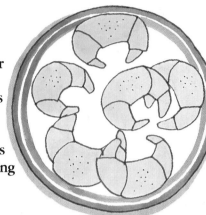

OPEN SANDWICHES

Open sandwiches can be endlessly varied and look very colourful and attractive. Don't overload the bread or the topping will fall off.

Marmite and cheese

Cress

Cream cheese

Carrot

Radish

Olive

Slice of cucumber

Shaped cheese slice on cream cheese

Round slices of cold meat

Beetroot

Cucumber

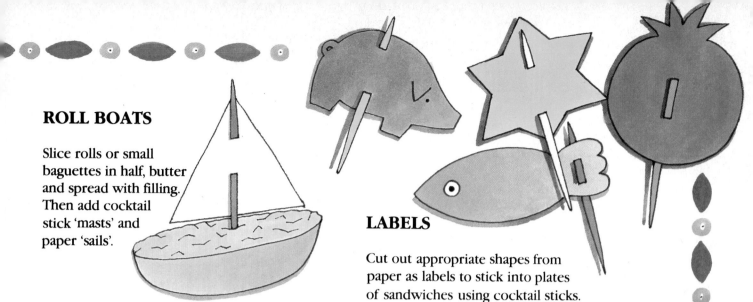

ROLL BOATS

Slice rolls or small baguettes in half, butter and spread with filling. Then add cocktail stick 'masts' and paper 'sails'.

LABELS

Cut out appropriate shapes from paper as labels to stick into plates of sandwiches using cocktail sticks.

SANDWICH HOUSE

A sandwich house is simple to construct and makes a fun centrepiece on the table. Cut square sandwiches for the main building, arranging them in a solid block as big as you like but not higher than three sandwiches or they will fall over. Cut triangular sandwiches for the roof, buttering both sides of the bread to help stick the sandwiches together (cocktail sticks can also be used to help secure the sandwiches). Cut vegetables for windows, doors etc.

Twiglets or cheese straws for roof →

Carrot Windows →

Carrot door →

SMALL CAKES

Bake lots of small sponge cakes. You can freeze them if you want to make them in advance.

SPONGE MIXTURE

To make about 16 fairy cakes you will need...

150g or 6oz softened
    butter or margarine
150g or 6oz caster
    sugar
3 eggs
150g or 6oz self-
    raising flour

Set the oven at 180°C/350°F/Gas Mark 4. Put the softened butter and sugar in a mixing bowl and beat with a wooden spoon until the mixture is pale and creamy. Beat the eggs separately, then add them to the butter and sugar mixture a little at a time, stirring well until smooth. Sift the flour into the mixture and mix well.

Spoon the mixture into individual paper cases and smooth level. Bake the cakes in the oven for 15-20 minutes until risen and golden brown.

CHOCOLATE CRISPIES

Chocolate crispies are popular with children, both to make and eat. They are very easy to make as no baking is required.

Simply melt some chocolate in a bowl, then stir in Cornflakes or Rice Krispies. Place large spoonfuls in cake cases and allow to cool and harden.

GLACÉ ICING

Glacé icing is easy to make and can be used to decorate cakes and biscuits. Sift icing sugar into a bowl. Add hot water a little at a time, mixing it with the sugar to make a smooth paste.

Use a wet knife to help spread it. You can add food colouring to glacé icing, or make a chocolate variation by replacing a quarter of the icing sugar with cocoa powder.

Colour glacé icing with food colourings.

BUTTERFLY CAKES

Make the fairy cakes as usual. Then, when cool, carefully cut a shallow hole out of the top of each. Fill the hole with butter icing. To make the butterfly wings slice the cut-off top piece in two and stick the straight edges together into the icing at an angle.

Butter icing

Wings

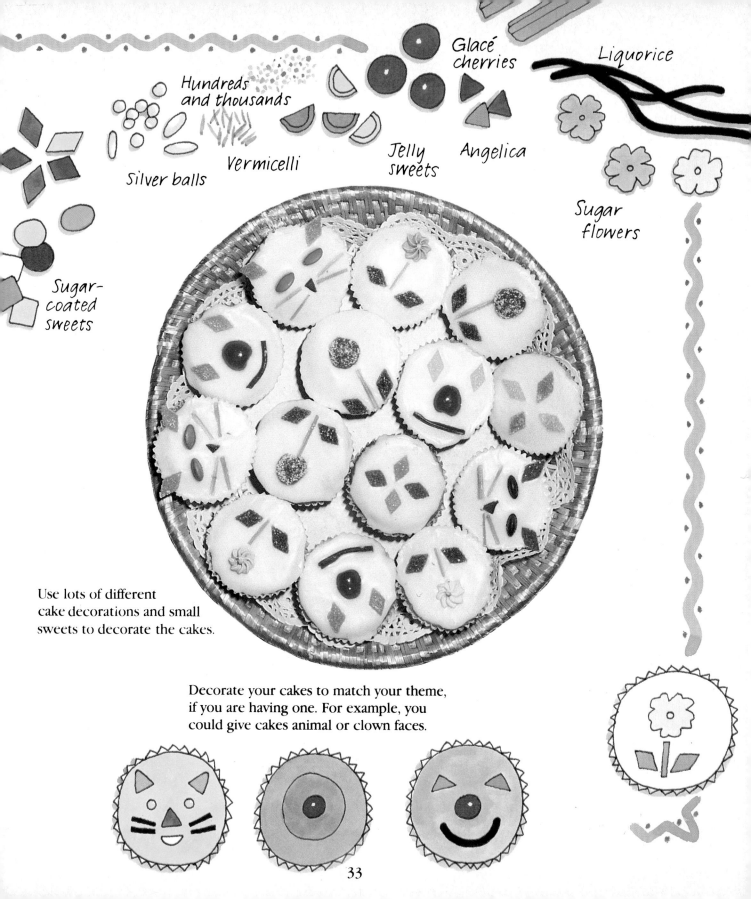

Hundreds
and thousands

Glacé
cherries

Liquorice

Silver balls

Vermicelli

Jelly
sweets

Angelica

Sugar
flowers

Sugar-
coated
sweets

Use lots of different
cake decorations and small
sweets to decorate the cakes.

Decorate your cakes to match your theme,
if you are having one. For example, you
could give cakes animal or clown faces.

33

JELLIES

Individual jellies in paper dishes are pretty. Make several different flavours. You can add a little chopped up fruit at the bottom and a blob of 'spray' cream on top.

A large jelly made in a mould makes an amusing centrepiece, though looks rather messy once cut.

Pink rabbit with 'mashed' green jelly around it on a plate.

MILK JELLIES

Melt jelly in hot water as normal, then top up to required amount with fresh or evaporated milk. For a striped effect, make half the jelly with water, leave it to set, then add a layer of milk jelly.

MAGIC JELLIES

You will need...

Large oranges
Packets of differently flavoured jelly

Cut the oranges in two and carefully scoop all the flesh out of the halves. Stand the empty skins on trays (use bits of Plasticine to help keep them upright).

Use bits of Plasticine or Blu-tack to hold up the fruit.

Use differently coloured jellies.

Then make up the jellies. Don't use quite so much water as instructed on the packet to ensure the jelly sets firmly. Pour the jelly into the orange skins up to the top. When set, carefully cut each orange half into three 'segments'.

The segments 'magically' have jelly inside the real orange skin. It's fun to make lots of different colours.

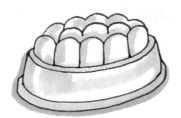

Look out for jelly moulds in different fun shapes and sizes.

Make jelly 'boats' using cocktail sticks and paper 'sails'.

Sea of mashed-up blue jelly

STRIPED JELLY

Set different coloured layers of jelly in glasses for a striped effect. Allow each new layer to set before adding the next colour.

JELLY KEBABS

Set differently coloured jellies in ice cube trays with the divider removed (or in a shallow plastic tray). Use slightly less liquid than instructed on the packet. Then cut the jelly into cubes and thread on to skewers.

DRINKS

If you want to be more adventurous with drinks than the basic juices, squashes and fizzy drinks, here are some simple recipes to try:

MILKSHAKES

You will need...

325g or 12oz fresh
 fruit
2 tablespoons caster
 sugar
900ml or 1½ pints milk
4 scoops vanilla ice
 cream

Place half the fruit, sugar, milk and ice cream in an electric blender or food processor. Blend for 20 seconds, then pour into a jug. Repeat with the remaining ingredients. This recipe makes 1.2 litres (2 pints) of natural, creamy milkshake. Serve in tall glasses with straws.

ICE CREAM SODAS

Fill glasses half full with lemonade, then add scoops of ice cream. You could use cola or cherryade instead.

FRUIT PUNCH

Top glasses of fruit juice up with lemonade. In the winter you could make a hot punch with blackcurrant drink, orange juice and water.

HOT CHOCOLATE

Marshmallows floating in hot chocolate make a delicious treat in the winter. Alternatively, spray cream on top of a hot chocolate drink and grate chocolate on top, or sprinkle on hundreds and thousands. Serve with teaspoons.

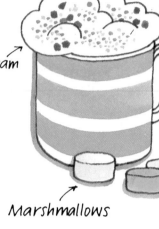

Cream

Marshmallows

HOMEMADE LEMONADE

For a refreshing and natural lemonade try this quick and easy recipe:

You will need...

4 lemons
75g or 3oz caster
 sugar
1.2 litres or 2 pints
 boiling water

Grate the rind from the lemons and place in a heatproof jug with the sugar. Pour over the water and stir until the sugar has dissolved. Squeeze the lemons and strain into the jug. Allow to cool. Makes 1.2 litres (2 pints).

MAGIC POTION

For a very fizzy effect, freeze chocolate drops and place a few at the bottom of each glass. Then fill the glasses with sparkling drink.

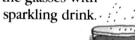

Put slices of orange and lemon on the rim of glasses.

Dip the rims of glasses in lemon juice, then sugar or coconut.

Make decorations for straws. Keep them simple and place near the top of the straw.

Tissue flowers

Butterfly

Names

Cleo

Tinsel

Paper fruit

Bat

Spider

PIZZAS

You can make pizza bases well in advance and freeze them. When ready to cook, cover the bases in a tomato sauce (see recipe below). All the additional toppings can be selected and added by the children at the party. Let them do this between games so the pizzas can be ready to eat from the oven when the meal starts.

PIZZA DOUGH

This recipe makes two 10cm (4 in) pizza bases.

You will need....

150g or 6oz self-
   raising flour
Pinch of salt and
   pepper
40g or 1½ oz butter or
   margarine
50g or 2oz grated cheese
3-4 tablespoons milk

Chop up the butter and place in a bowl with the flour and seasoning. Rub in the butter until the mixture looks like breadcrumbs. Add the grated cheese and the milk and mix it all together until you have a small ball of dough. Divide the dough in half and roll out into 10cm (4 in) circles. Once the pizza bases have been covered with tomato sauce and toppings, bake them for 15-20 minutes at 220°C/425°F/Gas Mark 7 until the edges are golden brown.

Have the bases already on baking trays if the children are going to decorate their own. To prevent the pizzas getting muddled up, you could get the children to make distinguishing marks in their decoration, or write their names on strips of greaseproof paper tucked under the bases.

PIZZA SAUCE

You will need...

1 small onion
1 small tin tomatoes
1 dessertspoon tomato
   pureé
Pinch of salt and
   pepper

Break up the tinned tomatoes with a fork and mix in the tomato pureé, (or put into a blender or food processor for a few seconds). Heat the mixture together with the chopped onion and seasoning for 15 minutes in a saucepan. Allow the sauce to cool before spreading on the pizza bases.

MINI PIZZAS

Crumpets or muffins can be used as bases for mini pizzas. Add tomato sauce and toppings in the normal way.

Individual mini quiches would also go down well. Bake them in pretty frilled pastry cases.

Names on greaseproof paper

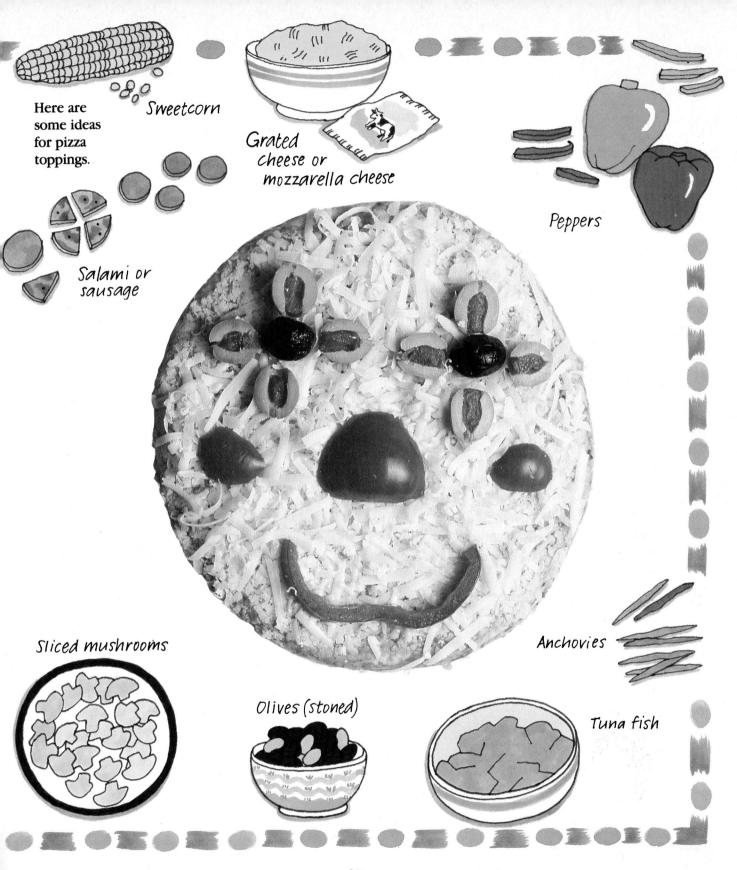

Here are some ideas for pizza toppings.

Sweetcorn

Grated cheese or mozzarella cheese

Peppers

Salami or sausage

Sliced mushrooms

Olives (stoned)

Anchovies

Tuna fish

FRUIT

Most children love fresh fruit. What you choose to serve obviously depends on the season. Tinned or frozen fruit can also be used. Many fruits are now tinned in their natural juice rather than syrup, and these are healthier.

FRUIT KEBABS

Dip small fruits, such as strawberries, grapes or tangerine segments, half way into melted chocolate. Leave them until the chocolate has hardened, then thread on to cocktail sticks to serve.

BANANAS

Bananas are especially popular with children. For a special treat, dip whole bananas in melted chocolate and then roll them in hundreds and thousands.

You can also bake bananas in their skins, either in the oven or in the embers of a bonfire, until the skins are blackened. Peel back a strip of skin when cool enough to eat and serve on a plate with cream and brown sugar.

Make sure the bananas are cool enough to serve.

TOFFEE APPLES

You will need...

14 short wooden sticks
14 medium dessert apples
675g or 1lb demerara sugar
75g or 3oz butter or margarine
2 teaspoons vinegar
175ml or 6fl oz water
2 tablespoons golden syrup

Push a stick firmly into the core of each apple. Heat the other ingredients gently in a large heavy-based saucepan until the sugar has dissolved. Bring to the boil and boil for 5 minutes, without stirring, until 143°C (290°F) is reached on a sugar thermometer, or until a little mixture dropped into cold water goes hard. Remove from the heat and stand in cold water to stop the mixture cooking.

You could wrap the apples in paper.

Dip the apples one at a time into the mixture. Lift each apple out and twirl over the pan until evenly coated with toffee. Place on an oiled baking sheet until the toffee has hardened.

FRUIT SALAD

Cut the top off a pineapple and carefully scoop out the flesh. Cut the flesh into cubes and mix it with other fruit. Fill the pineapple with the fruit. Keep in the fridge until ready to serve.

You could use a melon instead of a pineapple.

Pour a little orange juice over the fruit salad.

Lemon juice stops fruit going brown.

Cut large fruit into cubes or use whole small fruits. Put on to cocktail sticks and push into half a grapefruit or a large orange.

BARBECUE

Barbecues are fun either for lunchtime or a summer tea, or in the winter as part of a firework party. If you don't want to cook a lot, even hot dogs and warmed pitta bread will make a nice change and are easy to do. Afterwards the children can toast marshmallows. Remember always to have an adult in charge of the barbecue to avoid any accidents.

KEBABS

Cut chicken and pork into cubes and thread alternately on to metal skewers. For extra flavour, marinate the meat for several hours before cooking (see the recipe opposite).

Add vegetables such as cherry tomatoes, pickled onions and chunks of pepper for a bit of colour.

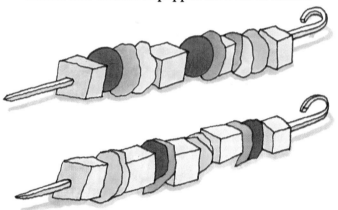

JACKET POTATOES

Cut baked potatoes in half and scoop out the insides. Mash them together with grated cheese and butter or margarine and spoon back into the skins. Garnish with cress, or use cocktail sticks and slices of cheese and pepper to make 'boats'.

MARINADE

HONEY AND ORANGE

You will need...

2 tablespoons clear honey
1 tablespoon Worcester sauce
Grated rind and juice of ½ orange
1 tablespoon tomato pureé
1 tablespoon soy sauce

Mix all the ingredients together in a bowl and brush over chicken drumsticks or any meat. Cover the meat completely in silver foil and marinate for at least 1 hour before cooking. Use any remaining sauce to baste the meat while it is on the barbecue.

PITTAS

Mini 'party' pittas are a good alternative to the normal burger buns as small children will find them fun and easier to eat. Warm them up in the oven first, then slit open one end and fill with salad, pieces of hamburger or vegiburger and slices of cheese. Serve with a paper napkin.

A BARBECUE CAFÉ

Write a menu on a blackboard or piece of card and serve your guests from a table.

Mini filled pittas, ready to serve.

Chestnuts are good to roast at the end of a winter barbecue. Eat them with salt and butter.

'PIG IN A BLANKET'

A 'pig in a blanket' is an original way to barbecue sausages or frankfurters. Wrap a couple of rashers of bacon around each sausage, leaving the ends sticking out. Use cocktail sticks to secure the ends. Cook over the barbecue.

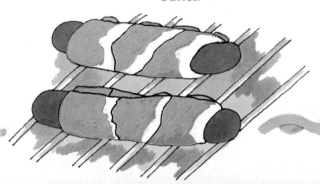

43

BISCUITS

Biscuits are very popular and easy to make. A tray of these in different shapes, iced and brightly decorated, is ideal for children to take into school on their birthday.

BUTTER BISCUITS

To make 20 biscuits you will need...

100g or 4oz butter or margarine
100g or 4oz caster sugar
1 egg
225g or 8oz plain flour
Rind from 1 lemon, finely grated

Set the oven at 180°C/350°F/Gas Mark 4. Cream the butter and caster sugar together until light and fluffy. Then beat in the egg gradually. Stir in the seived flour and lemon rind to form a stiff dough. Knead the dough lightly and roll out to 5mm (¼ in) thick. Cut into required shapes and place on lightly greased baking trays. Bake until a light golden colour. When cooked, place the biscuits on a wire rack to cool.

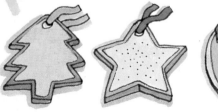

Make a hole with a skewer in the top of the biscuits before cooking. When cooked and allowed to cool, thread with ribbon or wool and hang up or give out as going home presents.

SPICY BISCUITS

To make 24 biscuits you will need...

275g or 10oz self-raising flour
1 dessertspoon of cinnamon
100g or 4oz soft brown sugar
75g or 3oz butter or margarine
1 small egg
50g or 2oz golden syrup

Set the oven at 170°C/325°F/Gas Mark 3. Sift the flour and cinnamon into a mixing bowl, then stir in the sugar, Cut up the butter and rub it into the mixture until it looks like breadcrumbs. Beat the egg separately with a fork and then add the golden syrup to it, mixing until smooth. Make a hollow in the flour mixture and pour in the egg mixture. Mix together until you have a big ball of dough. Place the dough in a plastic bag and keep in the fridge for 30 minutes. Roll out, cut, and bake as with butter biscuits.

Children will love to help cut out the biscuits in different shapes and decorating them by pressing chopped nuts, currants or sesame seeds into the dough. When cooked you can decorate with icing, cake decorations and sweets.

Using the spicy biscuits recipe, make gingerbread people and write the guests' name on them, using tubes of icing.

You could dip some biscuits half into melted chocolate.

Decorate the biscuits with jellies and sweets.

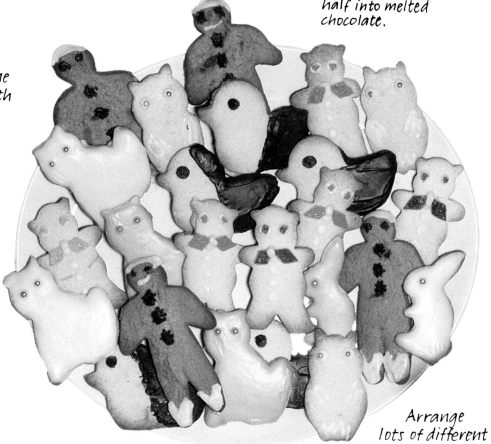

Arrange lots of different biscuits on a plate.

Make biscuits to match the theme of your party.

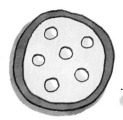

ICE CREAM

Most children enjoy ice cream. Whether you make your own or buy it, serving ice cream with a sauce makes it extra special for a party. These sauce recipes can be made a few days in advance and kept in the fridge.

BUTTERSCOTCH SAUCE

You will need...

284ml or 10fl oz carton double cream
100g or 4oz unsalted butter
150g or 6oz soft brown sugar

Place all the ingredients in a heavy-based saucepan. Heat gently, stirring until the sugar has dissolved. Then bring to the boil and boil for 2 minutes, until syrupy. Serve hot or cold.

MAKING SUNDAES

Put various flavours of ice cream, the sauces and as many toppings as you like out on a table so the the children can construct their own sundae. Try to avoid a mad scramble all at once, and have the table and surrounding area well covered! Alternatively, put single scoops of ice cream in ramekins or small bowls and decorate as faces or animals.

CHOCOLATE SAUCE

You will need...

150g or 6oz plain chocolate, chopped
50g or 2oz caster sugar
250ml or 8fl oz milk

Place all the ingredients in a saucepan and heat gently, stirring until the sugar has dissolved. Simmer for 2 to 3 minutes. Serve hot or cold.

RASPBERRY SAUCE

You will need...

150g or 6oz raspberries, frozen or fresh
75g or 3oz caster sugar

Wash the raspberries and push them through a sieve over a bowl using a wooden spoon. Add the caster sugar to the raspberry pulp a little at a time. Then stir the sauce vigorously until all the sugar has dissolved. Serve hot or cold.

MARS BAR SAUCE

For a very quick and delicious sauce, gently melt Mars bars in a saucepan with a little milk.

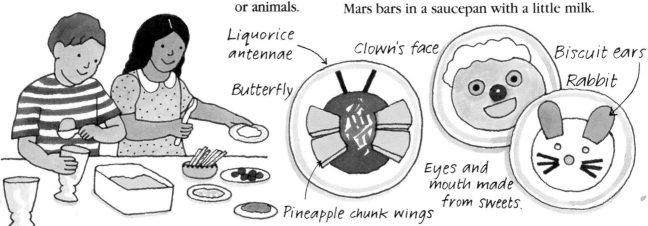

Liquorice antennae

Butterfly

Clown's face

Biscuit ears

Rabbit

Pineapple chunk wings

Eyes and mouth made from sweets.

Add a miniature umbrella for a final, fun touch.

Put all the toppings into small bowls or saucers with a spoon in each.

Chopped fruit, fresh or tinned

Vermicelli

Chocolate logs

Glacé cherries

'Spray' Cream is the easiest to use.

Cream

Hundreds and thousands

Chocolate drops

Chopped nuts

Wafers

Sponge fingers

Use thick glasses or glass sweet dishes if you can't get sundae glasses.

47

SALADS

Children can be very fussy about eating salad and fresh vegetables, so take extra care to present vegetables in a novel and attractive way. Make use of the naturally colourful varieties for decoration.

VEGETABLE SHAPES

Cut brightly coloured vegetables, such as peppers, carrots and tomatoes, into shapes and use to garnish plates of sandwiches. You could also thread chunks on to cocktail sticks to make vegetable kebabs.

VEGETABLE KEBABS

Vegetable shapes and small vegetables such as radishes look good threaded alternately on to skewers.

TOMATOES

Scoop the insides out of cherry tomatoes and fill them with cream cheese. You can have fun arranging the tomatoes in amusing and interesting patterns, for example the age of the birthday child.

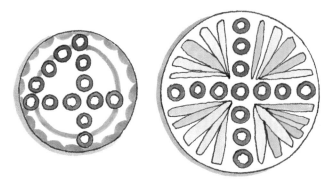

VEGETABLE DIP

Slice carrots, cucumbers, courgettes, and celery sticks into small, thin strips and serve with a dip. Avoid any strong or spicy ingredients. Try mixing cream cheese or peanut butter with yogurt, or tomato ketchup and salad cream or mayonnaise.

Party
CAKES

3·CAKES

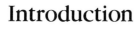

INTRODUCTION

If you are ever stuck for new ideas for children's party cakes - or are not sure how to make novelty cakes - then this section will help you. Everything here is straightforward to make, and detailed pictures clearly explain each stage. Your children will love helping with the cooking and decorating, as well as eating the results!

The easy basic sponge cake recipe on page 52 shows you step-by-step how to create fun and attractive cakes - for birthdays or other special celebrations.

The instructions show you how to create several variations of each basic idea. Following the same methods, you might like to try experimenting with some of your own ideas.

There are plenty of tips on decorating your cakes too, using fondant or butter icing with simple added extras, such as wafers and sweets. Always avoid using whole nuts and sweets that could get stuck in small children's throats.

Many of the cakes can be linked to a party theme, for example a space party or circus party.

Ingredients are given in both metric and imperial measures. It is best to use either metric or imperial, but not a mixture of both.

Natural food colourings are available. When you go shopping, look at the alternatives on offer and carefully check the ingredients. Annatto, riboflavin, cochineal and beetroot red are all natural food colourings.

At the end of this section there are several additional ideas for you to try. It might be a good idea to keep a 'Party' file of magazine cuttings for future use.

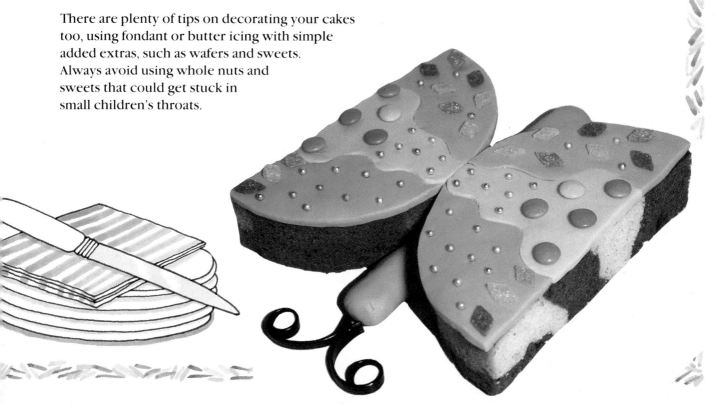

BASIC RECIPES

You will need . . .

2 x 20cm or 8in
round cake tins
150g or 6oz
    softened
    butter or
    margarine
150g or 6oz caster
    sugar
3 eggs size 3
150g or 6oz self-
    raising flour

Variations

Chocolate - add a
little hot water to
25g or 1oz of cocoa
powder and mix to a paste (or melt the same
amount of chocolate). Beat into the creamed
butter and sugar mixture.

Orange or lemon - finely grate the rind of one
orange or lemon and add to the cake mixture.
For extra flavour add a little of the juice.

Marble - divide the creamed mixture in half. Add a
little hot water to 25g or 1oz of cocoa powder and
mix to a paste. Mix into the creamed mixture. For
different colours, add a few drops of food
colouring and mix well. Place alternate spoonfuls
of the two mixtures in tins.

1   First set the oven at
180°C/350°F/Gas Mark 4.
Put the softened butter
and sugar in a mixing bowl.
Beat together with a wooden spoon until the
mixture is pale and creamy. Add the beaten eggs
to the mixture a little at a time, stirring well until
it is smooth.

2   Sieve the flour into the mixture and fold in
carefully until well mixed. The cake mixture
should be soft and light. Grease tins with butter or
margarine, add a little flour, shake, then empty out
(or use a pastry brush and a teaspoon of oil). You
could line deep tins with butter papers or
greaseproof paper. Pour half the cake mixture into
each greased tin and smooth until level.

3   The cake is done when well-risen and brown.
It should feel springy in the middle and be starting
to shrink away from the edge of the tin.
As an extra test, insert a warm
metal skewer into the middle
of the cake - if it comes out
clean then the cake is ready.
Turn onto wire racks to cool.

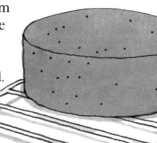

Butter icing

Butter icing can be used to stick cakes together, and to make a rough surface decoration. Use half the amount of butter to the amount of icing sugar (you can use margarine instead) e.g. 75g or 3oz of butter to 150g or 6oz of icing sugar. Beat the icing sugar into the bowl a little at a time, mixing in with the butter. If too thick to spread stir in a little milk. Use a piping bag to apply the icing, or a warm knife to spread it. As a less sweet alternative, make an icing from soft cream cheese mixed with lemon or orange juice and honey.

Fondant icing

Fondant icing is ideal for covering and modelling. Buy packets of 250g or 450g and roll out to desired thickness. Cover rolling pin with icing sugar first to prevent it sticking to the icing. When covering cakes, apply a little jam to the cake surface first to help it stick. Use your finger to mould fondant icing and cover joins, with a little water if necessary. To cover a pudding basin-shaped cake, roll out the icing into a round and then mould it round the cake. Keep fondant icing covered when not using it to stop it drying out.

Glacé icing

Glacé icing is very simple to make and covers cakes easily. Sift 150g or 6oz of icing sugar into a bowl. Add hot water a little at a time, mixing it with the sugar to make a smooth paste that is easy to spread.

Decoration

Cake decorations such as silver balls and plastic flowers, sweets, and dried or fresh fruit can all be used. Avoid whole nuts as these can choke small children. Marzipan or fondant icing can be shaped into figures.

Press different shaped objects into icing while it is still soft to form interesting patterns.

You can colour icing or marzipan by adding a few drops of food colouring and kneading well, or by painting with a brush after modelling.

Press fondant icing through a garlic press to make 'hair' and 'branches'.

BASIC CAKES

You can create all kinds of novelty cakes by cutting and building with the basic shapes shown below. Stick the pieces together with jam or butter icing.

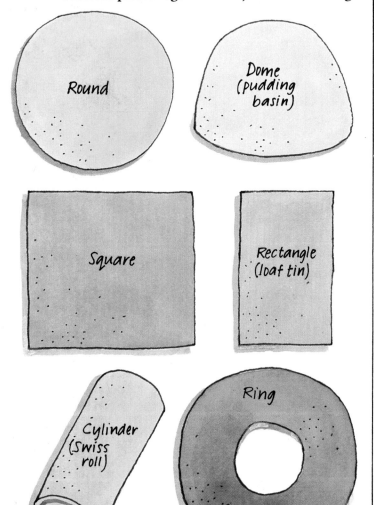

Small cakes, biscuits, ice cream cones and wafers are ideal for details such as ears and arms.

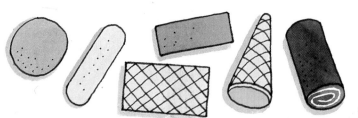

Here are two simple ideas from pieces joined together:

MONSTER CAKE

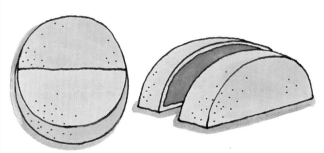

Cut a ring cake in two, slide along and stick together.

RAINBOW CAKE

Cut a round cake in two, stand up and stick together. You could cover the cake in fondant icing and paint stripes with a brush and food colouring. Or apply butter icing using a knife or piping bag.

NUMBER CAKES

Hire, buy or borrow the cake tins and use the same number of decorations on top.

Swimming pool

Use biscuit cutters to make fondant icing shapes for decoration. Sprinkle with cake decorations.

Keep models simple and bright.

Use ornaments as candle holders.

Shark fins would be fun!

If you have a party with a theme, it can be fun making a cake to match. Cover a simple shape in icing and model figures.

Chocolate logs topped with green icing make good trees.

Football

Start making your models early, a few at a time, and keep them in a tin.

Write a message with a brush and food colouring.

Ice skating

Happy Birthday

TOIL920

CLOWN

You will need . . .

1 x ½pt or 10fl oz
   pudding basin
   sponge cake
1 x 1pt or 20fl oz
   pudding basin
   sponge cake
2 x 250g or 1 x 450g
   packets of fondant
   icing
2 sponge fingers
1 ice cream cone
Food colouring
Sweets

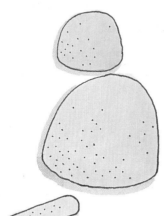

1   Colour and roll out 300g or 11oz of icing to cover the body and for sleeves. Roll out 100g or 4oz of white icing and cover the head and sponge fingers. Press the head and arms into the body.

2   Decorate the clown's body by pressing sweets into the icing. Use sweets to make a nose and eyes. For the mouth use a short strip of liquorice.

3   Colour the remaining fondant icing orange to make hair and cut into a fringe shape. Press carefully around the head. Cut the ice cream cone to fit the head and use as a hat.

Tom is 5 today!

WITCH/WIZARD

Use biscuit cutters to make fondant icing shapes for decorations.

Happy Birthday

Make a banner from a strip of paper and two small sticks.

Cover the clown's hat in fondant icing and decorate.

You could use a bought hat.

CASTLE

You will need . . .

3 x 180cm or 7in square
   sponge cakes
4 Swiss rolls
4 x 250g or 2 x 450g
   packets of fondant
   icing
Food colouring
Liquorice
Jam

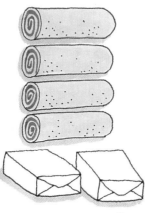

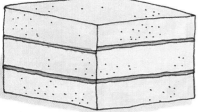

'Bite' cut out for a tower.

You could make the icing a sandy colour instead of grey.

1   Assemble the cakes in layers with jam. Cut 'bites' out of each corner. Add colouring to the icing, kneading well to mix. Roll out half of the icing and cover the cake.

2cm/ 3/4in

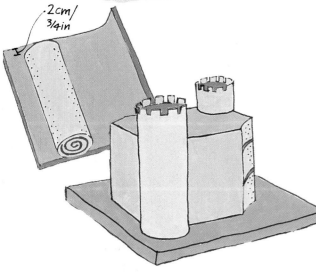

2   To make towers, roll out fondant icing to cover the Swiss rolls, leaving 2cm (¾in) spare at the top. Cut out squares from this, then cover each roll and stick them to the castle with jam.

3   Cut liquorice strips to make windows and a drawbridge and stick them to the sides of the castle with jam.

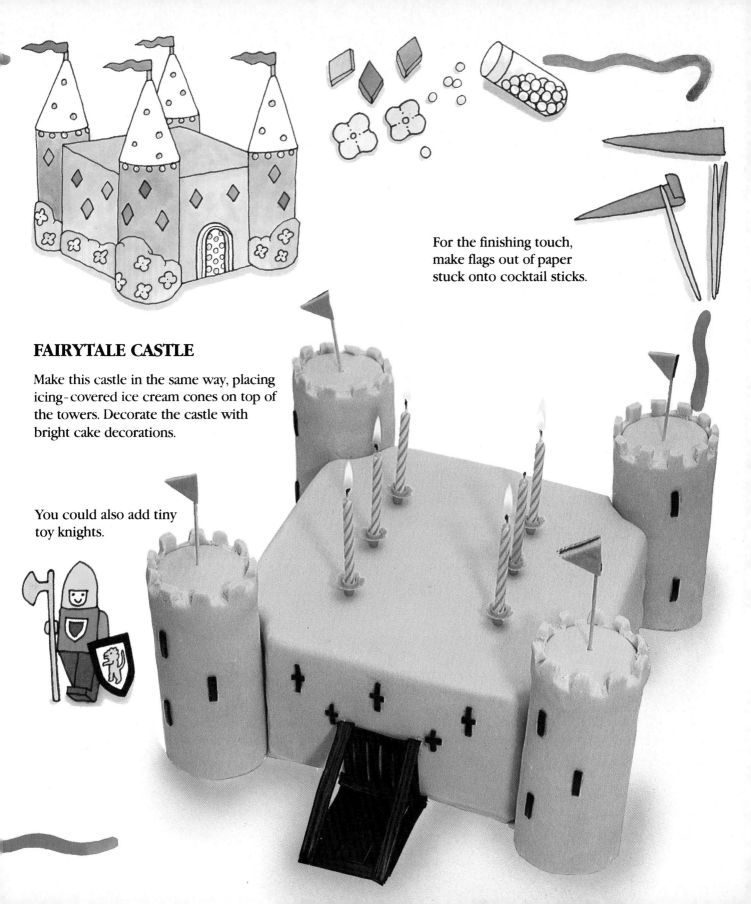

For the finishing touch, make flags out of paper stuck onto cocktail sticks.

FAIRYTALE CASTLE

Make this castle in the same way, placing icing-covered ice cream cones on top of the towers. Decorate the castle with bright cake decorations.

You could also add tiny toy knights.

RABBIT

You will need . . .

1 x ½pt or 10fl oz
   pudding basin
   sponge cake
1 x 1pt or 20fl oz
   pudding basin
   sponge cake
2 sponge fingers
200g or 8oz butter icing
Whipping cream
Brown or black
   food colouring
Liquorice sweets

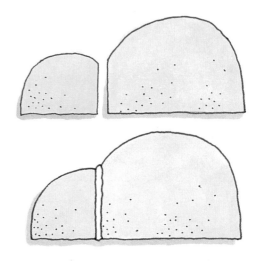

1   Cut a slice off one side of each cake and stick the cakes together using a little of the butter icing.

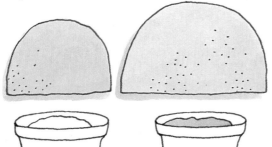

2   Divide the icing up and colour one batch. Use both batches to cover the body, using a knife or piping bag. Cover the sponge fingers and press in place on the cake.

3   Make the rabbit's face from sweets. But before serving, arrange a big blob of fluffy cream for a tail.

For a birthday you could place candles in holders and stick them along the back of the cake. You could model a carrot out of marzipan or fondant icing and place it next to the rabbit for a good finishing touch.

CAT

Wafer ears↓

Match your pet's markings if you have one.

Sponge finger tail ↓

MOUSE

Biscuit ears↓

Liquorice or string tail ↓

61

TEDDY BEAR

You will need . . .

2 round sponge cakes
4 mini Swiss rolls
230g or 8oz butter icing
Small amount of
    fondant icing
Yellow and red
    food colouring
Sweets

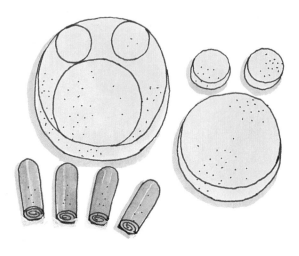

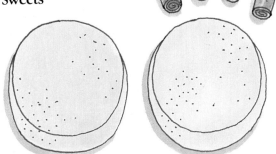

1   Cut one cake into a smaller round for Teddy's head and two little rounds for his ears.

2   Assemble Teddy's body on a tray or board. Stick all the parts together with butter icing. Colour the rest of the icing, and cover the whole body, using a knife or piping bag.

3   Stick on sweets or fondant icing to make eyes, nose and mouth. Colour the fondant icing, cut a bow tie out of it, and decorate with silver balls.

LADYBIRD

SUN

Use liquorice to make antennae and spots.

Surround a cake with sponge fingers and ice cream wafers.

PANDA

Make like the Teddy, but cover in black and white fondant icing.

Add candle 'buttons' down Teddy's tummy.

ROCKET

You will need . . .

1 Swiss roll
1 ice cream cone
6 ice cream wafers
2 x 250g or
    1 x 450g
    packets of fondant
    icing
Liquorice sweets
Blue food colouring
Small amount of glacé
    icing (optional)
Candles and holders
    (optional)

1   Divide the icing in half and add drops of colouring to one half, kneading well to mix. Roll out to about 3mm thick. Roll out the rest of the icing.

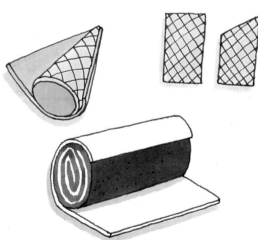

Decorate with sweets and liquorice →

2   Carefully wrap the blue icing around the ice cream cone. Cut one corner off each wafer. Cover the Swiss roll with white icing, pinching the edges to seal.

3   Assemble the rocket by standing the Swiss roll on end on a plate or board. Push the wafers in evenly around the base. Place the cone on top and pinch icing together.

64

To make a larger cake, add a smaller Swiss roll on top. Stick together with glacé icing.

If the rocket and candles seem unsteady, stick them to the base with glacé icing.

Push candles into holders and then into sweets. Place around the base.

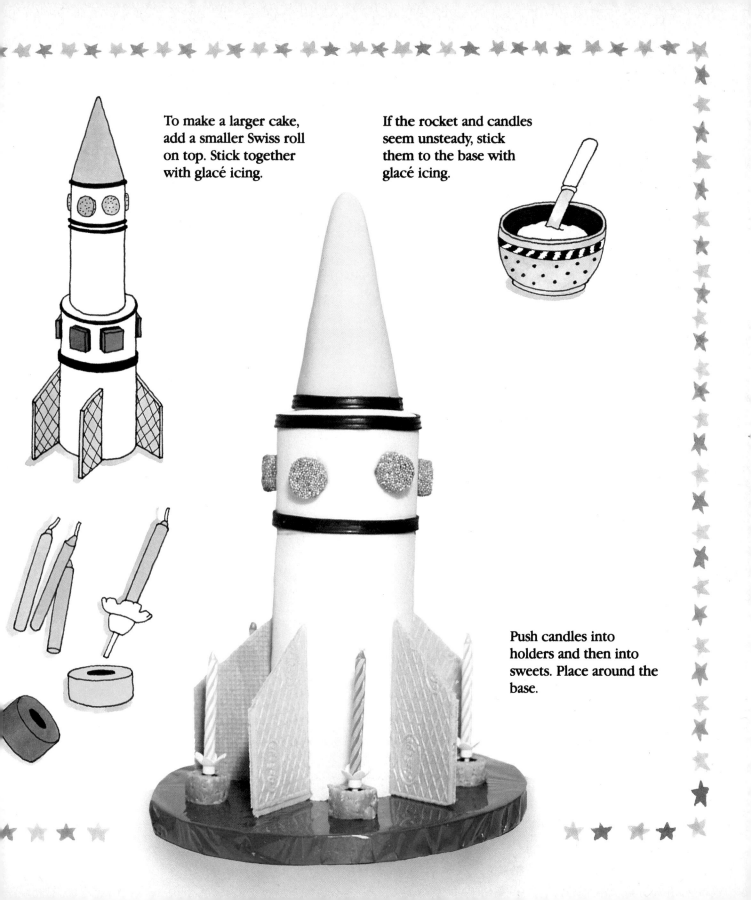

BUTTERFLY

You will need . . .

1 x 20cm or 8in round
  marble sponge cake
2 x 250g or
  1 x 450g
  packets of fondant
  icing
2 sponge fingers
3 food colours
Sweets, liquorice and
  cake decorations

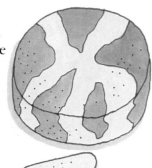

1   Cut the cake into two halves and put them back to back. Cut each sponge finger to fit as the body of the butterfly.

2   Divide the icing into three equal parts and colour each piece by kneading well with a few drops of food colouring. Roll out and cover the top of the cake and the sponge fingers.

3   Decorate the butterfly with sweets and pretty cake decorations. Make the antennae from pieces of liquorice.

BAT CAKE

You can add liquorice 'wing lines' if you like.

Follow the same instructions as for the butterfly, using a marble sponge cake and sponge finger. Cut three 'bites' out of the straight edge of each half of the cake. Place together, position body, and cover with black icing. Add icing ears and sweet eyes.

DINOSAUR

You will need . . .

2 round sponge cakes
2 sponge fingers
200g or 8oz butter icing
3 ice cream wafers
Sweets
Food colouring

Sandwich two cakes together with butter icing.

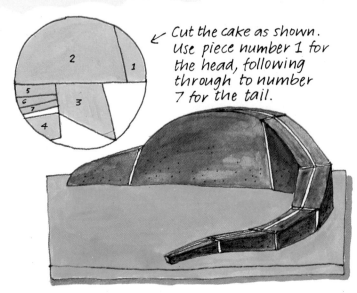

Cut the cake as shown. Use piece number 1 for the head, following through to number 7 for the tail.

1   Cut up the cakes as shown above, arranging the pieces into a dinosaur shape on a board or tray. Stick them together with butter icing.

2   Liberally cover the whole dinosaur with butter icing. Cut the sponge fingers in half and press into position as feet. Also cover these with icing.

3   Cut the wafers into three triangular pieces and stick them along the top of the dinosaur. Decorate with sweets, using two large ones for the eyes.

Make tiny trees out of green fondant icing and chocolate logs.

WHALE

Silver foil

Wafer teeth, fin
and tail

SHARK

Sharks, whales
and snowmen are
all easy to model.

Coconut
snow

SNOWMAN

Raisins
and
fondant
icing
details.

BUS

You will need . . .

2 x 2lb or 1kg loaf
    tin sponge cakes
2 Swiss rolls
2 x 250g or
    1 x 450g
    packets of fondant
    icing
Red and black food
    colouring
Sweets
Jam

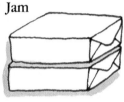

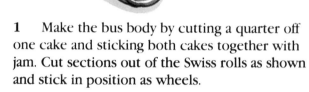

1   Make the bus body by cutting a quarter off one cake and sticking both cakes together with jam. Cut sections out of the Swiss rolls as shown and stick in position as wheels.

2   Colour 300g or 11oz of the icing red and roll out to cover the bus. Then colour 100g or 4oz of icing black, roll out and cover the wheels. From the remaining white icing, measure and cut a strip for the windows.

3   Stick sweets on for hubcaps and headlights. With any remaining icing cut out passengers, paint them with food colouring and press onto the windows.

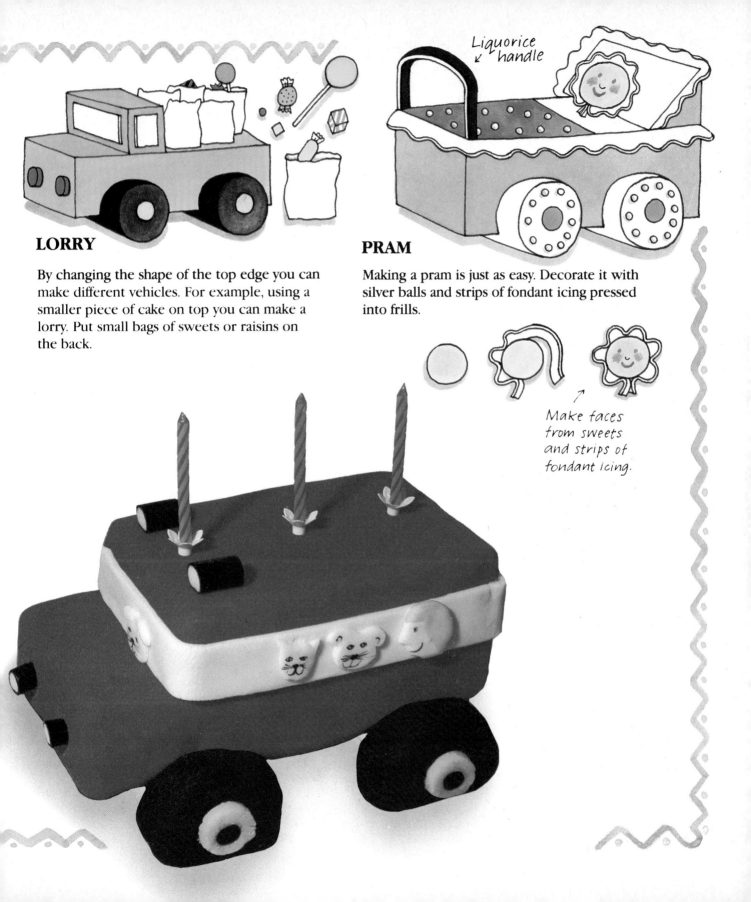

LORRY

By changing the shape of the top edge you can make different vehicles. For example, using a smaller piece of cake on top you can make a lorry. Put small bags of sweets or raisins on the back.

PRAM

Making a pram is just as easy. Decorate it with silver balls and strips of fondant icing pressed into frills.

Liquorice handle

Make faces from sweets and strips of fondant icing.

MORE IDEAS

Here are three more cakes easily made and decorated.

CATERPILLAR CAKE

You will need about 4 Swiss rolls for this cake.

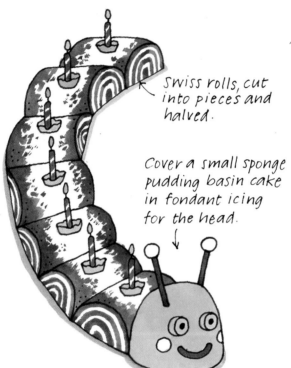

Swiss rolls, cut into pieces and halved.

Cover a small sponge pudding basin cake in fondant icing for the head.

CHEESE AND MICE CAKE

Buy or make sugar mice.

Use two quarters of a round sponge cake stuck together with jam or butter icing.
Gently press 'holes' into yellow fondant icing with the end of a wooden spoon.

TRAIN CAKE

Use mini Swiss rolls to make this cake.

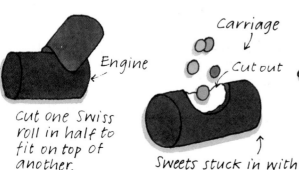

Engine

Carriage

Cut out

Cut one Swiss roll in half to fit on top of another.

Sweets stuck in with butter icing.

Liquorice or chocolate finger track

Make a carriage for each child.

Party GAMES

4 · GAMES

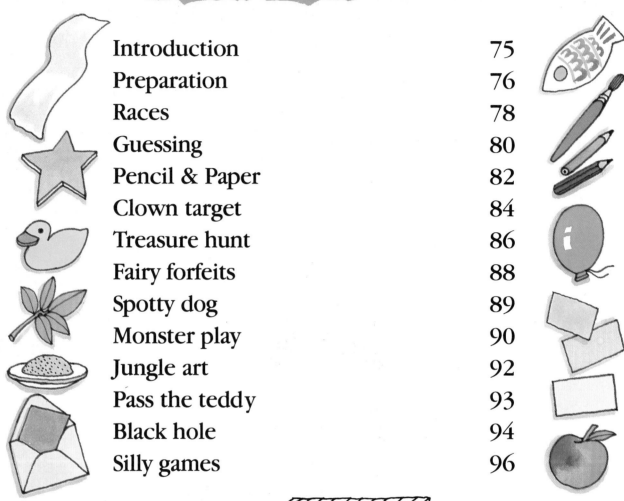

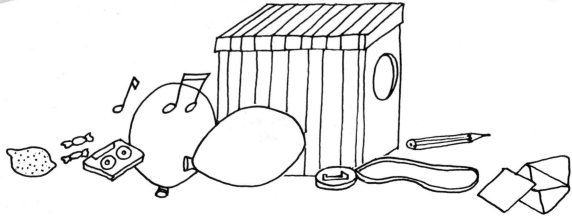

INTRODUCTION

Games are perhaps the most essential element of any children's party. This section is full of all sorts of different games - some you will recognize as variations on traditional favourites, while others involve you and the children in making novel props for games based on a theme, such as a 'black hole' for a space party.

Children need to release their energy running and jumping around, so there are plenty of races and musical games to choose from. Make sure you have enough space cleared indoors if you can't hold the party outdoors.

It's a good idea to intersperse these energetic games with quieter activities. You'll find the pencil and paper games, and guessing games, explained in this section are popular. Children also enjoy making or drawing things, especially if they can then use them afterwards in a game.

Some of the games are more suitable for younger children - some for older ones. Though most can be adapted for any age group as the basic rules are very simple. Many of the games are more fun when played in teams, especially if the number of guests is large.

PREPARATION

Be well prepared before the day of the party. It's a good idea to enlist some extra adult help on the day to set up each game in advance, so you avoid delays between games when children may get restless. Keep an eye on the time; starting off the party with games, serving tea in the middle, then having time for more games afterwards. If the weather permits, hold games outside for the space. If you are holding a party indoors, move furniture to the sides of your largest room and move anything breakable.

VARIETY

Try and alternate energetic, noisy games with quieter ones. However, if a game is particularly enjoyed and doesn't require a lot of setting up, for example races or musical bumps, don't be worried about repeating it. It may be a good idea to have some 'sitting down' games straight after tea so the children don't feel sick rushing around!

PLAN

Make a list of all the games you intend playing, in the order you intend to play them. Then split the list into two - the first half for games to play before tea, and the other half for after tea. Always have more games planned than you think you will need as it's difficult to judge how long each one will take. It is a good idea to try out any new games beforehand to ensure they will work.

GAMES TO PLAY
1. Jungle art
2. Spotty dog
3. Pass the teddy
4. Black hole
5. Treasure hunt
6. Guessing game
7. Forfeits

RULES

Whatever games you play, keep the rules simple and explain them clearly at the beginning. Take into account the age and sex of the party guests when deciding on the games. Whatever you decide, little boys and girls can be very determined if they decide they don't want to play a certain game!

JOINING IN

You often find that there's one child who feels too shy at first to join in with the others. Get them involved by asking them to help organize things to start with. Be careful about incorporating too many games where some people will have to 'sit out' as some children may get upset or become bored.

MUSIC

Make sure you have some music organized for your party. Children love to dance and jump around to popular tunes and many party games need music to play them properly. You can buy special party tapes for children, or you could make your own from the radio or records. Have someone in charge of the music.

PROPS

Have all your props together in a box - music tapes, small prizes, stop watch, and so on. You can make some of these beforehand with your child. Masks or badges are simple to make and you can suit them to a theme if you are having one.

PRIZES

Children enjoy winning prizes, but they needn't be expensive. Toy shops are full of little novelties, such as miniature packs of cards and bits of stationery. Small boxes of crayons are also popular. Try to avoid giving out too many sweets, especially before tea.

Pass the parcel is always a popular game to play. Rather than having just one prize in the centre, you could place a few little ones between other layers.

Crayons

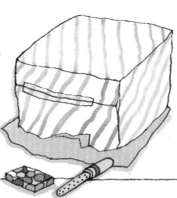

Badges or small toys

Rather than just giving a prize to the winner of a game, have some games where a team, or everyone taking part, wins something. If you are giving out prizes, it might be a good idea to put them in the 'going home' bags so the children can easily find them later to take home.

Emma

RACES

Races are better held outdoors, though some can be held indoors if the room is big enough. Clear away as much furniture as possible to the sides of the room and move anything breakable!

THREE-LEGGED

Divide the party guests into pairs and tie them together by the ankle (not too tightly) using old ties or rope. Hold relay races in teams.

WHEELBARROW

A wheelbarrow race is run in pairs. One person gets down on all fours, while their partner picks them up by their ankles. When everyone is ready in this position, they set off for the finish line - trying not to collapse!

RED ROVER

The more players you have for *Red Rover* the better. Everyone lines up on one side of the room or garden. One person is chosen to stand alone, some distance from the line. When he or she shouts "Red Rover all over", everyone must run over to the other side while the caller tries to catch someone. Whoever is caught joins the caller as the others run back the other way. Together they try and catch more people. Whoever is the last to be caught is the winner.

EGG & SPOON

Don't play this rather messy game indoors! Everyone lines up holding a spoon with an egg balanced in it. Whoever makes it to the finish line with their egg still intact on their spoon wins.

SACK RACE

Hessian sacks are the best to use for a sack race, though bin liners, potato sacks or old pillow cases are more easily available. Have a start and finish line. The best technique is to jump with both feet together, holding the sack with both hands!

Old pillow case

Plastic bin liner

FINISH

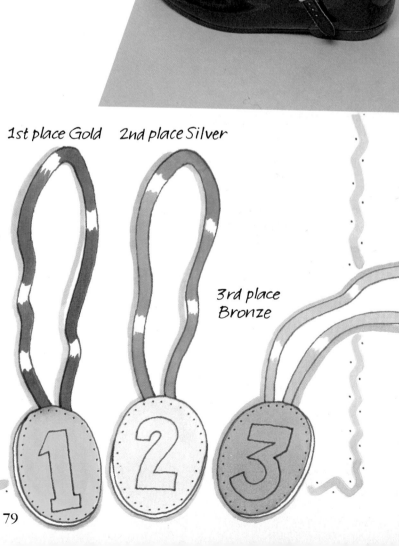

STEPPING STONES

Stepping stones is a simple but fun game. All you need are two sheets of paper per player. As each player steps forward, they must place a sheet of paper in front for their foot to step on to. Before they can step forward again they must lift up their back foot, pick up the piece of paper, and balance on one foot while placing the paper in front again. It's not as easy as it sounds, especially if you make it a team race!

MEDALS

The birthday child can help to make these medals to give to the winners of races and team relays.

Cut circles out of thick silver, gold and bronze coloured card.

Cut lengths of ribbon and tape the ends to the back of each medal.

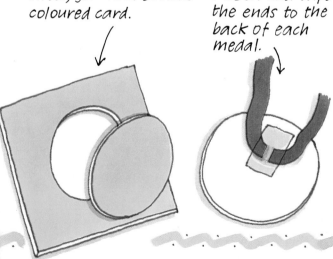

1st place Gold   2nd place Silver

3rd place Bronze

79

GUESSING

GUESS WHAT SMELL

Guessing games are always popular and make good competitions. To play *Guess what smell* you will need a blindfold and a number of 'smelly' items. Make some difficult, for example, a slice of bread, washing up liquid - and some easy, for example, a rose or coffee. Each player has one guess per item, for which they get one point if it's correct. Whoever gets the most points is the winner.

GUESS WHAT TASTE

This game is also played with a blindfold and involves guessing what things are by tasting them. Avoid too many strong tasting foods or players will feel sick! Try out sugar, salt, custard and cocoa powder. To make guessing more difficult, try various flavours of crisps or jams.

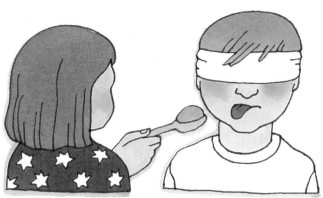

SQUEAK, PIGGY, SQUEAK

For this game, one person is blindfolded while the others sit around the room, preferably in soft chairs or on cushions. Whoever is blindfolded walks around the room and then sits down on someone's lap, saying "Squeak, piggy, squeak". Whoever they are sitting on starts squeaking, and the blindfolded person must try to guess the identity of the squeaker. If the guess is correct, the squeaker becomes the person to be blindfolded.

GUESS WHO

Guess who is played in pairs. The organizer writes down the names of famous people or types of animals on bits of paper and then pins one to the back of each player. One member of the pair then looks at the label on their partner's back and mimes that person or animal until the partner guesses who they are. They mustn't give spoken clues.

COW

Ideas:

Cow   Bird

Dog   Cat

Horse

Ideas:

Michael Jackson

The Queen

E.T.

Madonna

GUESS WHAT

You will need . . .

Cardboard box
Coloured wrapping
paper
Small household
objects

*Cover a cardboard
box with colourful
wrapping paper.*

*Place the objects to
be guessed inside.*

*Cut out two holes
in each side of the
box, big enough for
a child's hand to fit
through.*

Players take it in turns to feel the objects in the
box, writing down their guesses as they go along.
You could set a time limit to make it harder.
When everyone has had their turn, open the box
and check the lists to find out who got the most
guesses correct.

What objects you decide to put in the box will
depend on the age group of the children at the
party. Make most of them household items -
some hard and some easy.

For younger children you could use
a rubber duck, orange, toy car,
comb, teddy bear and sponge.

For older children you can have
more difficult objects. For example,
a woolly hat, playing card, paper clip, banana,
tube of toothpaste, pair of sunglasses,
sandpaper, roll of sticky tape.

PENCIL & PAPER

Party games tend to be noisy when there are lots of children, so it may be a good idea to include some quieter, less energetic games. This gives the organizers, and the guests, a rest! For most of the following games all you need to provide are pencils and paper.

LONG WORDS

To play this game you need to think of a long word, such as 'nightingale'. Players then have five minutes to write down all the words they can make out of 'nightingale', for example, 'night', 'gale', 'nail', 'gate' and so on. They must not be proper names. Count up the words. The winner is the person who has most words on their list.

LAST LETTERS

You can have any number of players for this game. Everyone sits in a circle. One person calls out the name of something. It can be a country, an animal, a vegetable or a flower. If 'daffodil' is called out, the other players must write it down and then try to think of a flower beginning with the last letter, for example, 'lilac'. Then a flower beginning with the letter 'c', and so on until everyone gets stuck. Count up each player's list of words. The winner is the one with the most words. With older children, you could play this game without writing the words down, just saying them out loud.

PICTURE WORDS

This is an amusing team game. Each person writes down the name of an object on a separate strip of paper, folds it up and places it in a hat or bag. A member from one team picks out a piece of paper and looks at the word. He or she then has one minute to draw the word. The other team members must try to guess what the word is. If they guess the word before the time is up, the team wins a point. Each team should have the same number of turns and the one with the most points at the end wins.

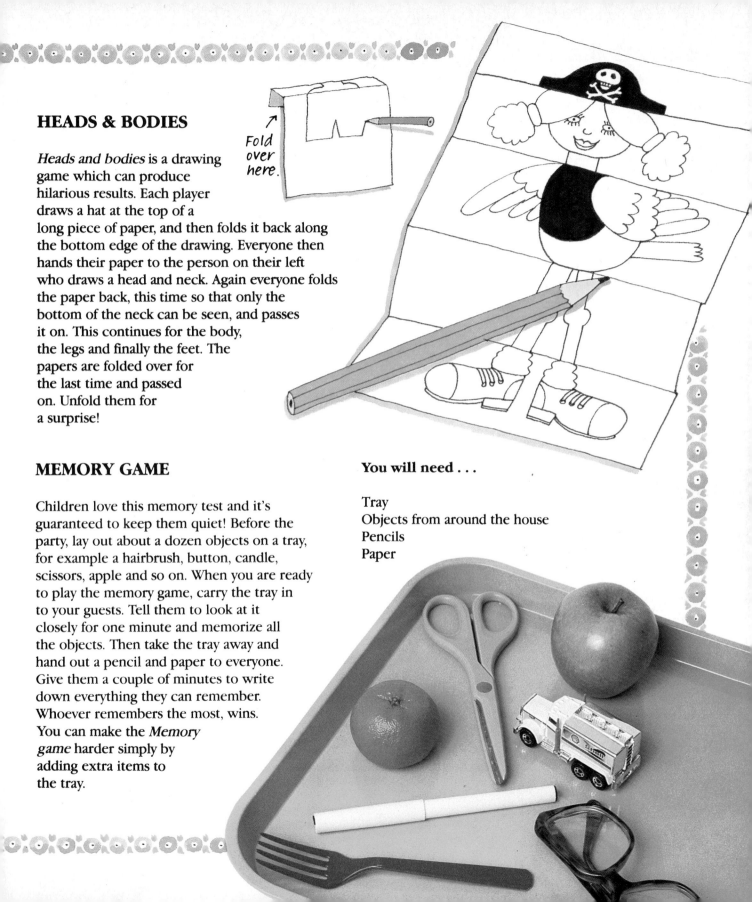

HEADS & BODIES

Heads and bodies is a drawing game which can produce hilarious results. Each player draws a hat at the top of a long piece of paper, and then folds it back along the bottom edge of the drawing. Everyone then hands their paper to the person on their left who draws a head and neck. Again everyone folds the paper back, this time so that only the bottom of the neck can be seen, and passes it on. This continues for the body, the legs and finally the feet. The papers are folded over for the last time and passed on. Unfold them for a surprise!

Fold over here.

MEMORY GAME

Children love this memory test and it's guaranteed to keep them quiet! Before the party, lay out about a dozen objects on a tray, for example a hairbrush, button, candle, scissors, apple and so on. When you are ready to play the memory game, carry the tray in to your guests. Tell them to look at it closely for one minute and memorize all the objects. Then take the tray away and hand out a pencil and paper to everyone. Give them a couple of minutes to write down everything they can remember. Whoever remembers the most, wins. You can make the *Memory game* harder simply by adding extra items to the tray.

You will need . . .

Tray
Objects from around the house
Pencils
Paper

CLOWN TARGET

Children will enjoy helping to make these targets as well as playing the game. The clown's face shown here was created with a circus theme in mind, though you could make a spaceman's head for a space party, and so on. This game is not recommended for younger children.

You will need . . .

Coloured card
Tissue paper
Scissors
Glue
Cocktail sticks
Blu-tack
Large straws

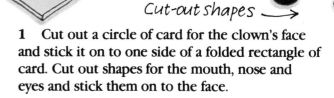

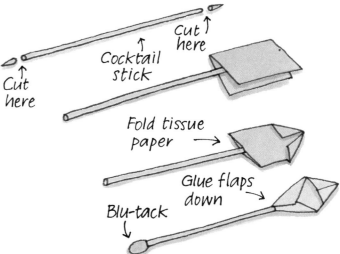

1 Cut out a circle of card for the clown's face and stick it on to one side of a folded rectangle of card. Cut out shapes for the mouth, nose and eyes and stick them on to the face.

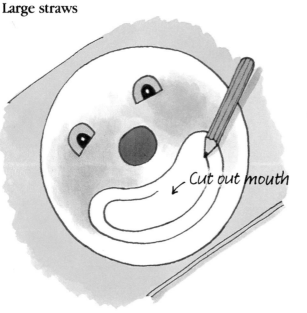

2 With a pencil, draw a line inside the mouth shape, leaving enough space to look like lips. Carefully cut out the rest of the mouth with a craft knife to leave a large hole.

3 To make the 'arrows', cut the sharp ends off cocktail sticks. Then stick a small blob of Blu-tack on one end and a tissue paper diamond-shaped 'tail' on the other end.

To fire . . .

Place the arrow, Blu-tack end first, down a straw, then blow hard down the straw, aiming to shoot the arrow through the clown's mouth.

Scoring

Make three arrows for each child and give points for direct hits. You could make a target for each child if numbers were small. Alternatively, make a couple of targets and hold competitions between teams.

WARNING:
Do not let
children aim
at each other.

Ideas for other targets.

Younger children could flip tiddlywinks into the clown's mouth, or throw Smarties from a marked distance.

CLOWN BALLOONS

Get the children to decorate balloons with clowns' faces. Draw a face using felt-tips or cut out shapes for eyes, nose and mouth from paper and stick on to a blown-up balloon. A good balloon game involves everyone standing in a line and passing the balloon, without using their hands, from one end of the line to the other. Play the game in teams. If someone drops the balloon it must go back to the beginning of the line again.

You could decorate balloons to suit other party themes.

TREASURE HUNT

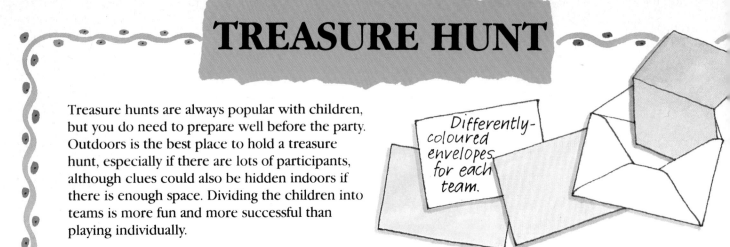

Treasure hunts are always popular with children, but you do need to prepare well before the party. Outdoors is the best place to hold a treasure hunt, especially if there are lots of participants, although clues could also be hidden indoors if there is enough space. Dividing the children into teams is more fun and more successful than playing individually.

Differently-coloured envelopes for each team.

You will need . . .

Pencil
Paper
Envelopes
Treasure

Depending on the number of children playing, divide them into at least two teams - Team 1, Team 2, and so on. The organizer then works out approximately ten different hiding places for clues. For example, if the hiding place is under a wheelbarrow, the clue for it could say 'The next hiding place is under something used for wheeling things round the garden'.

There should be a copy of each clue for every team. The last clue should lead the teams to the treasure, which the organizer hides before the start of the game. The treasure could be sweets or little toys. If you are having a theme party you could hide something appropriate, for example, chocolate coins at a pirate party.

Put each clue in a different envelope, marked with the number of each team, and leave them in the hiding places, apart from the first clue which should be handed out at the start. To avoid one team just following another to each hiding place, try and place each team's clues in a different order. The winning team is the one that finds the treasure first.

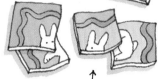

Old birthday card →

HUNT THE PUZZLE

Cut up old birthday or Christmas cards to make puzzles. One for each child or team. Or you could stick pictures from magazines onto thin card and cut up. Strong, clear images work best. Hide the pieces separately around the house. The winner is the one who completes their puzzle first.

Cut into several large pieces. ↑

FIND THE BURIED TREASURE

Younger children may find clues hard to follow, so you could try this buried treasure hunt instead:

You will need . . .

Paints or pens   Thin polystyrene sheet
Papers   Cocktail sticks
Scissors   Treasure

Draw a tropical island scene on a large piece of paper. Then cut around the island, leaving the top edge uncut so that it can be lifted up. Place the paper over polystyrene and, without the children seeing, mark an X on the polystyrene under the island. Each child must guess where the treasure is buried on the island by sticking in a flag (made from a cocktail stick and paper). Lift the island up to see whose flag is nearest the X. The winner is awarded the treasure.

NATURE HUNT

A nature hunt is a good idea if you can play in a park or garden. Give each child a list of things to find, some easy, some more difficult. Here are some ideas:

Twig
Leaves (various)
Stone
Feather
Flower (various)
Piece of litter
Seed

Paper or plastic bag

FAIRY FORFEITS

This forfeit game can be adapted to any party with a theme. This version has a fairy theme, so instructions are given to show you how to make a wand pointer board and lily pads with different forfeits written on the back. The rules are simple - each child sits on his or her own lily pad in a circle and takes turns in spinning the pointer. Whoever it points to when it stops has to turn over their lily pad and perform the forfeit. When they have finished they can sit out. The last person left in is the winner.

Forfeit suggestions:

- You have been turned into a frog - jump up and down 10 times.
- Run around the circle singing 'Ring-a-ring-of-roses.'
- Pat your head with one hand and rub your stomach with your other hand at the same time.

Lily pad

Wand pointer

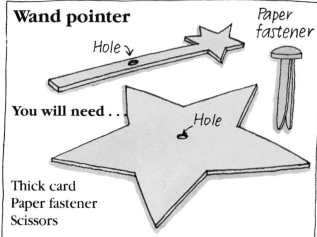

Hole

Paper fastener

Hole

You will need . . .

Thick card
Paper fastener
Scissors

Cut a giant star shape out of the card for the board. Then cut out a smaller star and a long strip (for the shaft of the wand). Make a hole in the middle of the wand and the board. Place a paper fastener through the holes, flattening out the prongs at the back. Don't secure it too tightly or the wand won't spin.

Lily pads

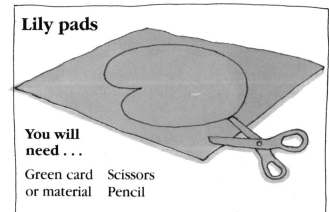

You will need . . .

Green card   Scissors
or material   Pencil

Draw a simple lily pad shape in pencil and trace it on to the green card or material, making one for each guest. Cut out the shapes. Then write a forfeit on the back of each pad (if using material, write the forfeits on paper and tape them on).

SPOTTY DOG

You will need . . .

Large piece of paper
Lots of small circles
of black paper or
sticky spots.

Pen or pencil
Blu-tack

For this game, you need to draw the basic outline of a dog and pin it to a wall. Divide the dog's body into areas, each scoring different points. Then stick a blob of Blu-tack to one side of the small circles of black paper. Each child is blindfolded and when it is their turn they are given several spots which they try to stick on the dog. If they miss altogether they get no points. At the end of each round add up the points to see who has scored the most.

MUSICAL SPOTS

With a 'spotty' theme in mind, try musical spots as a variation on musical chairs or bumps.

You will need . . .

Card, paper or material
Pen or pencil

Round object
Music

Use a large circular object to draw around on your card or material. Cut out one 'spot' for each guest and place them in the centre of the room. Play some music so the children can dance around the spots. When it stops they must sit down on a spot or they are out. Remove one more spot each time. Whoever sits on the last spot has won.

MONSTER PLAY

Children love to make things, so why not let their imaginations run riot making a monster! You could divide the children into teams and hold a competition to see who can make the best monster. It might be a good way to start a party by getting everyone involved. Start collecting suitable materials well in advance. The following items would make good basics which you can add to depending on what you have around the house.

Cartons

Cardboard tubes

Silver foil

Yoghurt pots

Coloured paper

Glue

Newspaper

Felt pens

Paints

Wool

String

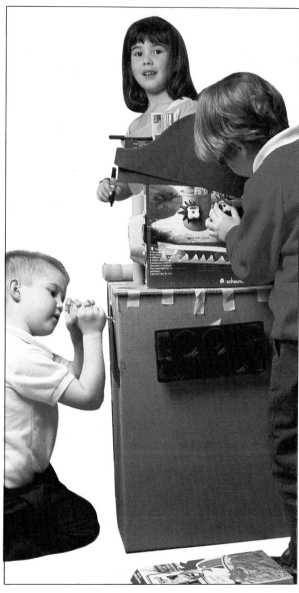

This is an activity that could be adapted to other party themes. For example, you could get the children to make an astronaut or a rocket at a space party.

MONSTER STATUES

For this game, children simply move around the room 'monster-fashion' to music, making suitable monster noises! When the music stops they must hold whatever position they are in for several seconds until the music starts again. Anyone who moves has to sit out. This is a game that could be adapted to other themes. At a jungle party, each child could pick an animal to imitate.

WHAT'S THE TIME, MIGHTY MONSTER?

Replace the traditional Mr Wolf character of this game with an equally menacing Mighty Monster. The more players you have, the more fun the game is. Whoever is chosen as Mighty Monster starts walking away from the rest of the players, who then start following him or her. Everyone together asks loudly "What's the time, Mighty Monster?". The monster can say any time it likes, but when the answer is "12 o'clock, dinner time", everyone must run back to the start. Mighty Monster runs after them and whoever is caught, or is last home, becomes the next Mighty Monster.

JUNGLE ART

Children love being able to create their own pictures, especially on a giant scale. Friezes and collages are often a good way of starting a party by getting the children involved from the moment they arrive. Some won't want to tear themselves away!

You will need ...
Rolls of old wallpaper
Magazines
Coloured paper
Pens or crayons
Scissors and glue
Sticky tape or drawing pins

You don't have to be an artist to start off a frieze. Just pin or tape wallpaper to the walls in strips and draw very basic outlines. The children will do the rest.

For a collage, it may be a good idea to cut out some shapes ready for sticking and colouring in or for drawing round.

Ideas for collage shapes

Children will enjoy drawing around each other posing in different positions. Make sure they don't draw too close to the person or it will mark their clothes.

Colour in the outlines in felt-tip pen or crayon.

PASS THE TEDDY

To play *Pass the teddy*, the children must stand in a circle. Start playing some music and give a teddy bear to one child. He or she then passes it to their left and so on around the circle, from person to person. When the music stops, whoever is holding the teddy bear is out. The last person left holding the teddy is the winner.

TEAM TEDDIES

Team teddies is a more difficult version of *Pass the teddy* involving more skill and more teddies! The children divide into two teams and stand in a line. Someone says "Ready, teddy, go!" and they start trying to pass a number of teddies down the line using any part of their bodies except their hands. If a teddy touches the ground at all, it must go back to the beginning of the line again. Whichever team first manages to get all their teddies safely to the end of their line, wins a prize.

BLACK HOLE

Combining luck and skill, this game is a space variation of the traditional indoor fishing game using fishing rods and magnets.

You will need . . .

Coloured paper (silver and gold)
Paper clips
Scissors
Sticky tape
Magnet
String and garden cane
Dustbin or bucket
Black plastic sack

1   To create a 'black hole', line a bucket or dustbin with a black plastic sack. You could decorate the outside by sticking on cut-out stars, planets and rockets.

2   Using the coloured paper, cut out stars, moons, planets, spacemen and alien shapes. Instead of using silver paper, you could cover shapes with tin foil.

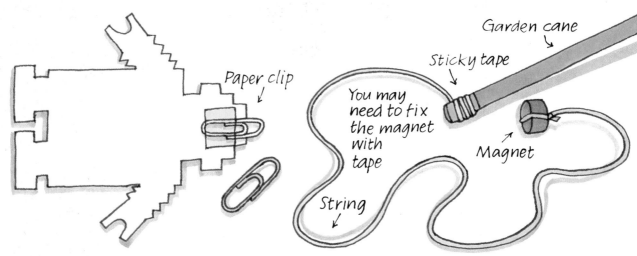

Garden cane

Sticky tape

You may need to fix the magnet with tape

Paper clip

Magnet

String

3   Attach a metal paper clip to the back of each shape using sticky tape, leaving enough metal exposed to attract the magnet. Place the shapes at the bottom of the 'black hole'.

4   To make the fishing rod, tie a piece of string to one end of a length of garden cane, securing it with sticky tape. Then tie a small magnet to the other end of the string.

VARIATIONS:

← You could paint a cut-down cardboard box to make a chest.

Tape paper clips to chocolate coins and paper parrots. ↙

Pirate

Use a basket or a wooden chest as a container. 'Fish' for chocolate coins and paper parrots.

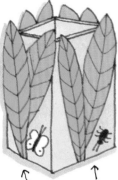

Jungle

Decorate a cardboard box with green paper leaves and 'fish' for paper animals.

↖ Paper leaves   ↑ Cardboard box

How to play . . .

You could hold team competitions, writing different points on the back of the different shapes to be 'fished' for. At the end of a time limit, add up each team's points to find the winners.

SILLY GAMES

There are some games that can only be described as 'silly', but children often find them the most fun!

SWINGING APPLES

This game is a race to see who can eat their apple the quickest. Use a metal skewer to make a hole through the centre of each apple. Then push a length of string through the hole and tie a knot. Hang up the apples at mouth height, then munch away!

SWEET BOBBING

This game will be very messy, so make sure you put down newspaper or an old sheet if playing it indoors. Put some sweets, such as marshmallows (avoid hard varieties that could choke children), on top of some flour or icing sugar in a bowl. The players take it in turns to kneel down and try to pick the sweets up without using their hands. Whoever manages to eat the most wins.

Produced by Times Four Publishing Ltd
Art and editorial direction: Tony Potter
Copy editor: Nicola Wright
Home economists: Nicola Berreen & Lycross Caterers

Kingfisher Books, Grisewood & Dempsey Ltd.
Elsley House, 24-30 Great Titchfield St, London W1P 7AD

This edition first published in paperback in 1993 by Kingfisher Books.
The material in this edition was previously published by Kingfisher Books in 1991 in four separate volumes under the series title *Children's Parties*.

10 9 8 7 6 5 4 3 2

Colour separations by RCS Graphics, Leeds
Typeset by C-Type, Horley, Surrey
Printed in Spain

BRITISH LIBRARY CATALOGUING IN PUBLICATION DATA
A catalogue record for this book is available from the British Library.

ISBN 1 85697 031 0